The Collected Yaps of
the Wee Ginger Dug
Volume 3

By Paul Kavanagh

Best wishes

Paul Kavanagh

Wee Ginger Dug Books

Published in 2016 by Wee Ginger Dug Books

Copyright ©Paul Kavanagh 2016

ISBN 978-0-9934057-4-7

A CIP catalogue copy of this book can be found in the
British Library and the National Library of Scotland.

Cover art by Maurice Rapallini

Dedication

To Peter, for showing that it's possible

to be happy again.

INTRODUCTION

This is the third volume of collected articles which were originally published on the Wee Ginger Dug blog, one of Scotland's leading political websites. The Wee Ginger Dug takes an acerbic and caustic look at Scottish politics, based on the principle that we need more mockery in Scottish politics because we have so much to mock.

This volume covers the period following the narrow defeat of the independence movement in 2014's independence referendum, and its regrouping and resurgence as the national awakening that refused to go back to sleep.

A Phoenix from the Ashes

20 September 2014

I t's time for the British Labour party in Scotland to end. Their party is over, their balloons bounce only because they are kept aloft by an alliance with big business and the City of London. British Labour wrapped itself in a Union flag and preached solidarity with the Tories and big business - remember that, never forget. There is no get out clause four, there is no devo-max or federalist jam. The solemn vow had evaporated long before it stained paper with the ink of the venal press printing machines.

Scotland must now refuse the worn out lies and brasso'ed necks of the Jim Murphys and the Magrit Currans - the man who whipped an egg up into a war, and the cereal woman who turns milk sour. Scotland must scoff at the platitudes of the visionless Gordie Broons and the Holy Wee Dougies - the one eyed man who made himself king by blinding his country with fear, and the creeping bejezuz of unchristian charity. They have used us long enough. Their victory will be pyrrhic.

There is no Scottish Labour party. There is a British Labour party which labours only to manage your expectations and keep the bosses happy. Every time they say that their name is Scottish Labour, they lie to you.

Scottish Labour is nothing more than a brand label on a tin that contains Conservative policies. It's a party whose great One Nation slogan is ripped off from 19th century Tories - British Labour is the backward looking clown face of progressive politics, a tape worm in the swollen belly of a Victorian working class child.

I'm proud of my city, Glasgow the city of Labour's birth, and proud of those throughout Scotland who saw through the deceit and voted Yes. The referendum campaign was the Thatcher moment for the British Labour party in Scotland. British Labour's cradle has rejected its accursed changeling child. It will be rejected and despised.

British Labour's party is over, but a new party is about to begin. One of the lessons to take from the second Scottish 45 is that the SNP alone cannot bring about independence. The idea of a single party leading a nation to independence belongs to the past century and in this modern age leaves the independence movement open to easy attack. It was all about Alicsammin. Or it will all be about Nicola Sturgeon or whoever takes over now that Alex Salmond has gracefully bowed out. The wider aims of the independence movement were lost in media attacks on SNP policies which the rest of us do not necessarily support. We cannot win an independence campaign if we all must agree to the policies of a single party. It must be a broad based coalition, and be seen to be such.

I have great respect for the achievements of Alex Salmond and the SNP for bringing the referendum about, and for opening Scotland to the opportunity to allow her diverse voices to talk, to sing, to laugh and debate. It's because of them that we are here, and for that they are due our sincere thanks and recognition. But we need a party which can find its support amongst those on the left, those of us who do not consider ourselves nationalists but independentistas, those who have been alienated from politics. People who would never support the SNP.

One of the dreams I held and still hold for independence was a Scottish Labour party that really was a Scottish Labour party, a Scottish people's party that was really a Scottish People's Party. Independence was the magic key that would open the door. But now in the aftermath of the Second 45, I see that we can't wait for independence in order to bring that party about. We must build our Scottish People's Party now. It is a precondition of independence.

We must ensure that pro-sovereignty parties dominate in Scottish politics. It is only by reducing the British Labour party to an insignificant rump that we have the best chance of a future Holyrood with a majority of pro-sovereignty parties. We must replace Westminster's useless windbags with MPs whose allegiances lie only with a party in Scotland and who will not sell out Scotland's interests. We must punish those who stood outside supermarkets and grinned ear to ear after David Cameron called on his pals in the boardrooms to scare Scots with higher prices.

Common Weal people, Labour for Indy, left wing SNP people, peace campaigners, anti-poverty campaigners, Greens, Socialists, RIC activists, LGBT rights activists, disability rights groups - we need to band together and found a new Scottish People's Party. A party firmly on the left, a party that is the true heir to the Scottish radical tradition co-opted and traduced by the British Labour party. I willingly offer my services as a lippy bastert for the cause.

Our hopes have been scorched and torched by the parasites of British Labour for too long, but a phoenix shall rise from the ashes.

An Open Letter to Magrit Curran

22 September 2014

I wasn't going to blog anything today, but I read in the Scotsman that Magrit Curran is to head a British Labour party commission which plans to visit the 10 areas of former British Labour support which returned a high Yes vote in order to discover why we turned our backs on Magrit's beloved career ladder. British Labour is asking us to put our trust in them once again. They have no shame, they have learned nothing, and now they look to us for answers to a problem of their own making and expect us to solve it for them so they can get back to business as usual, so they can pretend that nothing has happened.

No doubt the commission will operate as British Labour always operates, behind closed doors and talking to no-one except those who have been pre-approved. It is a window dressing exercise, a sham with no intent except to pretend to listen. It is a lie, like the very name "Scottish Labour" is a lie. British Labour does not listen, it only orders, it only commands, it only directs, it only takes. It is a creature of Westminster, not a child of Scotland's working class communities. British Labour sold out the working classes of Scotland for party interests, it exists to keep us trapped in hopelessness.

So as a former British Labour voter, who was brought up and lives in one of the working class areas that was lost to British Labour, I'd like to tell Magrit why we reject them, because she will not be soliciting my opinion, she will not ask to speak with me - or you. We are not pre-approved, and we will never approve.

We are not coming back to you Magrit. Your empty words are meaningless. We did not turn our backs on you, you turned your back on us. You have made your choices, and now we have made ours. We choose to repay your contempt with rejection, we choose to reject your platitudes with our passion, we choose to stand against you for you have chosen to stand apart. We are the people, not you, and you do not speak for us.

We see how quickly your vows evaporate. How little you offer. There is no place for you in our struggles, for you stand with the Tories, with big business, with the banks, and you wrapped yourself in the Union flag and grinned when the forces of the powerful threatened the community you claim to represent. You have bequeathed us a land where foodbanks are protected by nuclear missiles, and you tell us we can expect nothing better. You offer austerity, you offer loss, you offer disappointment. You offer to manage our expectations on behalf of the bosses. And the only gains that can be made are those which benefit the Magrit Currans, the Party people who put party before people.

British Labour has become nothing more than a career path for the ambitious, a chance of fame for the talentless. The British Labour party is the parliamentary tail of the Labour movement, the arse that thinks it's the brain and heart. The movement continues, the movement moves on. It must move on without British Labour. We have excreted you Magrit. You will be flushed away, unmourned.

Look forward to a future of exclusion Magrit. Embrace your rejection, it is the only comfort you will find. There is no place for your tribalism amongst the alliance of Yes. You have nothing to offer us, and all we have for you is to show you the door. Leave. There is no place for you amongst us. You do not belong here. You belong with the Tories, you belong in the boardrooms, you belong with those who play party games with people's lives. The only message we have for you is to tell you to fuck off back to your focus groups.

You are a nationalist Magrit, a British nationalist. You can reject the label but it will forever stick to you. The rampaging Loyalist mobs who sought out Yes voters to attack and assault in the wake of the vote, they are your people and your responsibility. The selfish ones who were asked to think of their country and the future of us all but who thought only of their nice shiny motors, their i-pads, their foreign holidays. They are your people, the materialists and the shallow ones. You represent their pinched faces, their pursed lips and their poverty of spirit.

This is a whirlwind of your own creation Magrit, and it will blow you away like the lifeless dust your party has become. There can be no reconciliation with your kind. Even Ramsay MacDonald once had principles, the great betrayer was a better human being than you and your and your party have become. The current generations of British Labour have never known principles. No soul. No heart. No love. You are dead to us because you are dead to yourselves. I will not reconcile myself to your corpse of hope, to the rotting stench of your decay. You will never put the coffin lid on my aspirations and dreams.

British Labour has been a long time dying. The last drops of red had dripped from its veins long before the referendum campaign began. Now all that is left is a rotting cadaver and a bad smell. It must be cleared away. If you wish to understand why we reject you Magrit, you do not need a commission. You do not need reports that will lie unread and undigested. You only need to look in a mirror. You are the problem, not us. We are the solution.

British Labour has made its choices, and now we make ours. Magrit and the rest of the British Labour party, we choose a future without you in it.

Being Irrelevant

28 September 2014

Yeah! We're irrelevant again. So we had this wee referendum thingy and Scotland scared the shiters out of the Westminster establishment - which was a lot of fun - and the UK media and political classes have gone back to ignoring us in the hope we don't go away. Now they're far too busy talking about UKIP, English devolution, and starting World War Three to bother themselves over much about Scotland. And there was me thinking that George Robertson had told us that it would be Scottish independence that started that. I must have missed something. Anyway, Scotland now gets to sit unobtrusively at the back of the class watching World War Three start without it being our cataclysmic fault, and we can plot how escape the clutches of the Westminster system without anyone paying us too much attention, which is pretty much the situation we've been in for the past 30 years.

So, you may recall - because the UK media doesn't - that a vow was made. It was a lovely vow, splattered all over the front page of the Record like one of those fake manuscripts you can buy at the market that assures you in wedding invitation lettering that everyone possessing your surname, like Kavanagh, Krisztowski or Kapoor, is a direct descendant of Robert the Bruce, William Wallace, and that guy that invented asphalt. Printing it like that just showed how serious the vow was, like a vow Buddhist monks make, only without any of the troubling obligations demanding self-denial, telling the truth, and not copping bad karma from the electorate. The one about the orange bedsheets is strictly observed however, because they can be claimed on expenses and you can get lovely Egyptian cotton ones from John Lewis.

I did say during before the referendum that I never knew independence campaigns could be such a laugh, and we really needed to have more of them. Looks like I'm going to get my wish. Pity it has to involve killing people. But hey, they're Middle Easterners. Perpetual warfare and killing Middle Eastern people is a British tradition, like bunting, royal babies, and swearing a lot whenever Nicholas Witchell comes on the telly. If Westminster had made a vow to Scotland to take military action against Nicholas Witchell instead of some Middle Eastern country I'd probably have voted No.

But back to the death, devastation, hubris, bleeding, weeping, and suffering, or the 'action' as the testosterone fuelled commentators on the telly refer to it as though it was a species of video game and not the destruction of human life. Yes, it's the Tory party conference.

The conference started today in Birmingham. Far from strutting the stage as the saviour of the Union, poor wee Davie is having to fight off defections to UKIP and a sex scandal involving some minister no one has ever heard of. It's not even a very juicy sex scandal, as no fishnet stockings, orange segments, orgiastic encounters with a Guardsman in Regents Park, or regimental goats played any part in it. It used to be that apart from kicking the working classes in the balls - but that's a given - the one thing you could rely on the Tories for was juicy sex scandals. They can't even do those properly anymore and it's really not good enough. At the very least they could make sure their sex scandals involved shrubbery. It's just tiresome sleaze these days, and we can get that from the British Labour party.

But the sex scandal is the very least of Davie's woes. Despite their rubbish sex scandals, the Tories have still managed to screw themselves, and look set to do to themselves in England what British Labour has managed to do to itself in Scotland - pissing off their core voters to such an extent that they desert them in droves. In the Tories' case, the pissing off has been done with the force of a water-cannon, and not that of a flaccid wee dick - although I promised not to say that about Ed Miliband. Voters in England have been driven in their desperation into the welcoming arms of the grinning Nigel. Another Tory wonder that we all wonder who the hell he is has defected to Nige's mob. At least in Scotland we have something noble to vote for instead, and many of us have the fake vellum manuscript from the market to prove it.

Just over a week after the referendum, and the Tories have joined British Labour in the waiting room for the express train to perdition. Divided, fractious, and trapped between the conflicting demands of the electorates in Scotland and England, the only reason they're still hanging around is because they privatised the railways and the service is as rubbish as the sex scandals.

British Labour in Scotland is equally too busy for vows, as it is currently preoccupied with in-fighting between those giants of Scottish politics, Johann Lamont and Jim Murphy, who are fighting over the chance to be chief undertaker in a party of corpses.

Johann's contribution to Scottish public life was eloquently summed up in a Tweet from Sean Bell, honest the cheque's in the post: *Every time I see Johann Lamont in action, I'm reminded there's a Scotmid somewhere without an assistant manager.*

And then there's Jim, the hero who bravely faced down an egg and shouted at old ladies. As a dedicated Blairite, Jim's chances of advancement within a shadow cabinet headed by Gordie Broon's former henchpersons are about as good as Magrit Curran's chances of ever actually swallowing that wasp, so all of a sudden he's remembered Scotland exists as an opportunity for him to build a power base within the party for himself. Johann's determined to organise the staff rota so Jim's on permanent back shift. Jim has the advantage here, as he makes a more convincing looking undertaker. And as a big fan of Tony Blair and an enthusiastic supporter of the war in Iraq - both the last one and this one - he's got previous experience.

The vow drops rapidly down the list of important things-to-do that fill the lives of our political leaders. It's now dropped below devolution for Yorkshire and reform of the 1863 Regulation of Mechanical Tin Plate Sex Toys Act, and is currently plummeting below "should I buy the orange sheets or the peach coloured ones". Though it has to be orange, that's the colour that really suits Labour and means they'll match the only friends they've got left in Scotland.

Meanwhile, us lot, the defeated, the hauden doon, and the beaten, the ones who are supposed to be bewailing our lot, rending our clothing and tearing out our hair, as we sit in the gloom besmeared with the ashes of our dreams, we're not following the script at all. Scotland has seen the membership of the SNP soar through the roof to over 70,000 and rising, membership of the Greens more than double, that of the SSP treble, and proposals are floating about to create a new Yes Alliance to hoover up the rest of the Yes voters and ensure a pro-sovereignty majority of Scottish MPs in 2015. So much for bayonetting the wounded then. The wounding of the British Labour party and the Tories has only just begun.

Dunno about you, but I'm feeling pretty smug already. The Unionist parties are the ones who are heading straight to irrelevance on a one way ticket. See - we told you so. It's the new national catchphrase.

The Nectar is Mince

1 October 2014

Ruth Davidson, who's abseiling all over the Tory party conference in Birmingham this week enjoying her fifteen minutes of relevance, has made the startling claim that the Conservatives might consider the SNP as potential coalition partners if the Tories don't win an outright majority. There are a number of possible reasons why the Action Krankie has thrown the last apparent shreds of reason to the wind bags:

A) She's delusional.

B) She's desperate for a bit of publicity because self-promotion is the only thing she loves more than kick-boxing.

C) She has a vastly inflated sense of her own importance, and that of Scotland within the Union.

D) She is genuinely unaware that the SNP have a long standing policy of not voting on non-Scottish matters, and an equally long standing policy of voting against nuclear missiles and foreign wars and so aren't about to prop up any UK government which needs support to get laws passed in England.

E) She is so lacking in self-awareness that she really doesn't appreciate the visceral loathing that the vast majority of independence supporters have for her party. It's a bit like Baron Frankenstein telling his house guests from the Guardian that the parade of peasants with pitchforks and torches is just the village fête.

F) She is genuinely clueless as a political strategist. No, really - dumb like soup, the kind without the pasta letters so you can't even spell out the words HELP ME.

G) She's paying back a wee favour to British Labour in Scotland by subtly associating the SNP with the Tories in order to shore up the Labour vote in Scotland and forestall SNP gains in the 2015 GE because even she knows that the Tories have fewer chances of taking a Labour seat in Scotland than there is of Gordie Broon getting through a political campaign without intervening frequently, each time for the first time.

H) All of the above.

My money is on H.

Back in the real world. For a given value of 'real'. Sarah Smith is just after telling us on thon programme that no one watches but me and I only watch to mock, that Gordon Brown has thrust himself into the constitutional debate again. I wish she wouldn't use that word in connection with Gordie. The notion of Gordon Brown thrusting himself is far too unsettling, and I've just eaten. I'll never be able to look at a buttered scone in the same light again.

The thrusting in question is that Gordie has started a petition, asking us to pledge him to vow about the vow he made a few weeks ago of behalf of Davie, Ed, and the other one who's even less relevant than Ruthie. It's terribly clever, just like Gordie. It's a meta-vow, a vow about a vow. It's one of those terribly clever things that only Gordon understands - like he's clever enough to understand the law of language that says if you lard your speech with incomprehensible Greco-Latin jargon phrases then you sound much cleverer than you really are. Because if you're really clever then you know how to explain it in language that everyone can get. Except the offside rule, but that's only because like somewhat over 50% of the population, I don't give a toss and zone out as soon as the words foot and ball are uttered. Gordie loves his Greco-Latin jargon phrases, like "endogenous growth theory". Which these days is how he has to say "I put an end to boom and bust", so that people don't titter.

Unfortunately Gordie's Latinate vocabulary problem has now jumped up and bit him on the steatopygia, because Gordie and the prono media - which is my new favourite word for the unionist media because it's just a finger slip away from porno - spent the last few days of the referendum campaign telling all and sundry we were going to get federalism and devo-max. Gordie and the prono papers studiedly refuse to pin these Latinate terms down like dead butterflies in a display cabinet so we could all have a good squatch and tut disapprovingly. And then we got a vow.

The big difficulty here is that terms like federalism and devo-max are not arcane and obscure phrases of holy writ whose correct interpretation can be determined only by those who have been anointed by the British Labour party with the power of infallibility, they've been a part of the common discourse of Scottish politics for many years longer than Gordie has deigned to pay attention. Most of us have a pretty good idea of what we think devo-max or federalism should mean, and these other notions don't necessarily coincide with Gordie's.

Any sensible definition of federalism would have a sensible answer to the Gagauzia Question. That's the question - how come an autonomous territory of 160,000 people in the poorest corner of Moldova, the poorest country in Europe, can have their own national TV network but Scotland can't? Any sensible answer to the question why income tax can be devolved at a rate of 15% but not 50% would have to give a sensible answer to the question of why all taxes can't be devolved. Or at least as many as those enjoyed by a small municipality in properly federal states, never mind a Swiss canton. And these questions would have to be answered in language everyone can grasp, without resorting to Latinate phrases that have no appreciable meaning. That's not going to happen.

So instead of *Lepidoptera caledoniensis thrawnbastertus* having its tartan wings frozen in the Westminster box of dead butterflies, we've got butterflies flapping about all over the place. And the butterflies are saying things like, "Why does the 'settled will of Scotland' have to wait for England to have a conversation about devolution for Yorkshire," or, "Show me a federation where the members don't have their own telly network," and, "Gordie, yer nectar's mince."

All this is going on even as the timetable for the enhanced devolution which has still not been defined or determined slips ever further down the Westminster political agenda. Yet this was the vow that Gordie swore he was going to ensure that the Westminster party leaders adhered to. It was a done deal. Now Gordie's asking us to sign a petition to get Gordie to enforce the vow. Sadly, he'd forgotten he was no longer prime minister. The done deal is done for and always was.

He's belatedly realised that he's the fall guy and his petition is a desperate attempt to make voters blame anyone but him for the impending debacle. Gordie asking us to sign a petition to get the Westminster party leaders to agree to do something he already got them to vow to do can only mean that Gordie doesn't trust the very same people that he asked us to trust. Bet you he won't explain that one clearly either.

Upstaged by an Autocue

2 October 2014

I've been watching parts of the Tory party conference. Not much of it, as the human body is only so strong and watching the entire proceedings would take at least four packets of imodium and a ball gag to stop me screaming swerry wurds. Even, I'm ashamed to say, the one starting with c and ending with t. But even that one doesn't feel strong enough, and Scottish lefty viewers of Conservative conferences are left with the appalling realisation that the English language is inadequate to the task. Davie Cameron is a fracking oleaginous clapped out bell-end, and the only reason he's not a wanker as well is because he's so useless he's incapable of doing anything for himself.

OK. I've got that out my system now. A detox session is vital after watching a selfishness of Tories - that's the proper collective noun in case you were wondering. You get George Osborne announcing tax breaks for better off pensioners - Tory voters - telling us with his narrow lips that individuals are the best judges of how to spend their money. Vote for me, peasants. And then you get Iain Duncan Smith, the man who makes Lex Luthor seem like Mahatma Gandhi, saying that the poorest families on benefits will no longer get all their income in cash that they can be the best judges of how to spend. They'll get prepaid cards that can only be used to purchase set items. Poor people who aren't a core Tory voting group need to have their spending decisions made for them by Iain Duncan Smith. Iain Duncan Smith is an anagram of 'dun in maniac shit'. That's probably significant.

On Wednesday we had Davie's keynote speech. They're called keynote because yer average Westminster politician could just sing through the musical scales repeatedly and impart the same information content. Conference pledges have the same relationship to reality as Gordie Broon. But what he did vow, because they're all very keen on vows these days, was 'English votes for English laws'. This is also a vow to unvow the vow that he vowed to Scotland, but vows made to non-Conservative voters don't count, and no one is going to lose any sleep over losing the parliamentary support of David Mundell. It's like the Rebel army losing an Ewok, only not as cutesy.

English votes for English laws is a slogan which has caught the headlines in a way its logical partner - Scottish votes for Scottish laws - never could. The prono papers have never troubled themselves over much with Scotland getting what it votes for. However England must always get what it votes for at all times and under all circumstances. This is only democratic. Scotland doesn't get the same consideration. But hey, we voted No. So we get what we're given and we lump it now that the option of leaving it has been taken off the table along with the cereal.

Labour has taken the humph, not so much because Davie's entirely predictable move screws over the expectations of Scotland, but because it screws over the British Labour party. British Labour is not going to stand for that kind of affront, not to their own power and influence. What's really bugging them is that a legal prohibition on Scottish MPs voting on English laws in effect creates two tiers of MP. Scottish MPs who cannot vote on key government policies which only affect England would be unlikely to hold any major offices of state. No more Scottish prime ministers. Anything that gets in the way of a British Labour MP and a career opportunity is terribly bad for democracy.

The worst of it is that one or other of this sorry bunch of shiny egos are going to be the next government.

The Sarah Smith Stardust Show had a detailed and incisive forensic examination of what all this means for the vow, which consisted of some shots of the Action Krankie at the Tory party conference looking smug because she got to sit next to Davie's missus, followed by Jackson Carlaw assuring us that it was all just fine and not to worry our silly wee heids because the Conservatives are utterly committed to delivering loads and loads of devolution goodies. All of which was uttered with the same conviction and self-belief as US Civil War general John Sedgewick, whose last words were allegedly an attempt to rouse his beleaguered troops into action by shouting "The Confederates couldn't shoot an elephant from this dist.... "

It was that subatomic exploration of the issues that we've come to know and love from BBC Scotland. Like when scientists looked very closely at the structure of the atom and discovered that what seems to be solid consists largely of empty space and very little matter. So it was quite appropriate really. No wonder Pacific Quay management is so pleased with its referendum coverage.

This was followed by Newsnight for Grownups with a package from political editor Allegra Stratton giving a summary of all the important points to be taken from Davie's speech. Allegra is concerned with the Big Picture, not that parochial subatomic stuff. She mentioned the UKIP problem, she mentioned the EU problem, she mentioned the promise to protect NHS spending, she spent an inordinate amount of time talking about Davie's latest tax cut wheeze, and she even found time to point out the importance of the autocue and how Davie used it to avoid the oops I forgot that £1.5 trillion deficit faux pas Ed Miliband committed when he gave his keynote conference speech - the one with the bum notes. There was nae mention of any tartan related vow in wedding font lettering. Not even the English votes for English laws one never mind the Scottish one. And Gordie Broon's petition doesn't rate a mention anywhere, and neither does Gordie.

So it's official. Scotland has less importance for UK party politics than an autocue. Probably that's because autocues only say what they're told to and someone else writes their script.

But here's an ironic wee factoid. In 2007 when Gordie Broon launched his leadership campaign at the British Labour party conference, he managed to deliver the entire speech with the autocue obscuring his face. They do say history repeats itself, and for the second time in his life Gordie has been upstaged by an autocue.

Labour, Wonga Puppets, and the Moral High Ground

3 October 2014

So it's a final farewell to the poll tax. Well, I say "farewell", when "consigned to the bin where it always belonged" is more appropriate. The Scottish Government has announced that local authorities can no longer chase up people for outstanding poll tax debts, debts which date back 25 years. It's a wee ha ha get it up yese from a departing Alicsammin to the British Labour cooncillors who were rumoured to have been heard licking their lips as they relished the prospect of punishing the poor who had turned against them.

Labour cooncils are beelin, because they had decided to use the increased voter registration in order to penalise people who registered in order to vote in the referendum, despite the fact that everyone, their granny, their granny's dug, and even their granny's dug's British Labour cooncillor, agrees that the poll tax was malign, unwanted, and unjust. It's better for the party when people don't bother to vote. British Labour understands this as contented aquiescence and not alienated despair. But now large numbers of people are once again engaging with politics, and this threatens to reveal just how hollow the party's apparent dominance in Scottish Westminster seats really is.

Making the lives of the poorest even harder in order to punish them. It's the typical small minded vindictiveness that we've come to know and love from the British Labour party as they complete their transition to a fully fledged right wing party, proponents of the belief that there can be no representation without taxation. They've become the party of net curtain twitchers, tutters, tskers, and the very worst small minded Presbyterian self-righteousness straight from the Victorian kailyaird. The British Labour party in Scotland has turned into the Sunday Post. It's even got Daphne.

But that's unfair. The Sunday Post had the graphic talents of that genius of ink, Dudley D Watkins. British Labour scrawls on the backs of fag packets. In lipstick, it appeals to women voters. Dudley D drew fantastic imagescapes of the Scottish imagination. Labour draws the blank look of Johann and the bankbook of Blair.

David O'Neill, president of Cosla, was raging about the poll tax soor grapes ban. There are fewer things more amusing to watch than a pursed lip in search of a pout. David ranted that it was "the oddest decision ever to come out of the Scottish government". Odder than Jock McConnell's decision to wear that kilt, odder than Jock's decision to allow Westminster to keep its paws on £1.5 billion because he couldn't think what to spend it on, odder even than North Ayrshire cooncil's decision to sign contracts to spend almost £430 million in PPP payments for new schools that cost £88 million to build. David O'Neill, leader of North Ayrshire cooncil, has a peculiar definition of oddness, but then he's a British Labour timeserver.

25

David moaned that no one had consulted him about it before the decision was announced. Because it's only right and proper in the odd world of British Labour that when you want to slap down uppity wee gits who are on a bigger power trip than a car park attendant during a bus strike, you tell them about it beforehand in order to allow them to get their excuses in first so they can appear pre-pouted in the TV studio.

Naturally, this doesn't hold if the car park attendant uses his or her awesome power to ban Audis, which is merely an act of social and moral responsibility. This is because Audi is German for "I have a very small penis and a need to over-compensate."

The news about Labour's shock and dismay at being refused the right to chase after ancient debts with the zeal of a witch-finder general came on the same day that pay day loan company Wonga announced that it was writing off £220 million in outstanding debts owed by thousands of clients who never had any realistic chance of repaying, and who never should have been given loans in the first place. Wonga has promised to change its business model and check clients' ability to pay before authorising a loan, and has issued an apology for the distress its lending behaviour has caused. British Labour in Scotland has less of a social conscience than a pay day loan company. That's jaw dropping, but admittedly only in a universe without Johann Lamont or Jim Murphy in it.

Our universe is far odder than that. We live in a universe where the puppets in the Wonga advert can lecture Labour from the moral high ground. And these are the people who claim to be the political heirs of Mary Barbour and the Glasgow rent strikes. Labour no longer believes in peacefully challenging authority in order to defeat an injustice. They believe they are the authority, and for a very long time they went unchallenged. That's changed now.

Over the course of the past few years, I've come to the distressing realisation that I loathe the British Labour party in Scotland even more than I despise the Tories, and it's not because I've got any more right-wing. It used to be common knowledge, by which is usually meant something that everyone believes because no one has ever bothered to contradict it, that people get more conservative as they get older. Apparently it's something that occurs naturally to humans once they discover that they have a use for a nasal hair trimmer. However, this hasn't happened to hundreds of thousands of people in Scotland, many of whom do have suspiciously hairy nostrils now that I come to think of it.

The Labour party hasn't aged at all well. The British Labour party has suffered an explosive outburst of nasal hair which has propelled it rightwards more quickly than a missile over Baghdad. It's the self-serving sneeze from those whose nasal hair is rooted in a nose in the trough.

During the referendum campaign independence supporters were lectured by certain supporters of the Union for our supposed fixation on the "narcissism of small differences". Insisting that Scotland is a different political space to the rest of the UK is an example of such narcissism, they told us. But there is no greater example of the narcissism of small differences than is to be found in the British Labour party and its attempts to portray itself as something different from the Conservatives. The party has wholeheartedly adopted privatisations, PPP schemes, foreign wars, benefits caps, and austerity cuts.

And now we have discovered that a pay day loan company has more of a conscience about the effects of aggressive debt pursuit on the poorest in society. I wonder what Mary Barbour would have said.

Garden Gnomes and Koalas

6 October 2014

I was going to blog something about the Lib Dem conference which was held in Glasgow this weekend, but what's the point? Does anyone actually give a toss what Vince Cable thinks? Even the rest of the Lib Dems don't care. You do better blogging about the minutes of the last meeting of the Auchterarder Market Gardens and Allotments Association summer outing subcommittee, which unlike the Lib Dems has a purpose and is at least going somewhere. Other than serving as enablers so one or other of the twin Tory parties can continue to take buggin's turn as the government of the day, the Lib Dems have no purpose, and most likely no future either.

But since the Auchterarder Market Gardens and Allotments Association are far too important and weighty and Scotland voted No so we aren't allowed to talk about important stuff, the Lib Dems will have to do. Their conference can be summed up in three sentences: What a pointless waste of time. Can I get the last 48 hours of Danny's Alexander's life back please. I'd like to do something inventive with them.

The Lib Dems vie with Gordie Broon for the title of Biggest Suckers in British Politics. It is only Gordie's recent masterclass performance in being taken for a mug that has pushed them out of pole position in the rankings. They can't even win at being losers. Gordie has been vowed the trophy, which he achieved during the final days of the referendum campaign by turning the word ego into a verb, only to discover that he'd been strung along like an overpuffed balloon and then burst by Davie Cameron's wee prick. It was the biggest explosion of a bag of noxious gas since Gordie mistakenly chose the beans during that fateful dinner with Tony Blair.

However Lib Dem party strategists have clearly decided to fight the General Election campaign on a platform of: We really hate the Tories too. No honestly. They're beastly. We said so all along, under our breath while Michael Gove wasn't listening. They bullied us into supporting them, they really did. It wasn't our fault. We'll support Labour if you like.

Despite the delusional nature of their self-belief, the Lib Dems maintain a cheerful disposition, founded entirely upon the proposition that come 2015 everyone will forget that Danny Alexander has spent the past five years as George Osborne's suppository. Danny has found his calling as the greasy slime which permits the smooth passage of Osborne's parliamentary motions.

And then there's that vow that a lot of people are itching to pay them back for. No, not the Scottish one. The tuition fees one that lasted as long as it took to say ministerial motor. Though that wasn't a vow, if memory serves it was only a solemn pledge signed in blood. Or in Menzies Campell's case, formaldehyde.

But even the harshest critic would have to admit that the situation is not entirely dire. The Lib Dems have escaped most of the blame for Gordie's disemvowment, but that's only because we already have Nick Clegg's tea oot for the student loans thing and being a second rate Tory when the original version was third rate to begin with.

Yesterday saw Wee Wullie Rennie and Alistair Carmichael launch into a fearsome attack on the SNP, which is like being savaged by an elderly and toothless Yorkie and its chew toy.

Wullie has given the SNP a wee test, because he's learned how to do them after someone showed him how to put a wee tick in the multiple choice box. And if he got it right he got a smartie. That's how he got the job as Lib Dem leader in Holyrood - well that and the fact there was no one else left.

Wullie said that the SNP and independence were like Gollum and his precioussssss, which he would know a lot about, since he had a non-speaking part in the fillum as a garden gnome. I always thought he was wasted in politics. Wullie has a face that you usually see in a DC Thompson cartoon, like the offspring of Daphne and Desperate Dan, and he could have a weekly series of misadventures and homespun philosophy with his pal Alistair the prissy Koala in the pull out section of the Sunday Post. It would at least add to the sum total of human happiness in a small but significant way.

Instead he's wasting his enormous natural talent on making up a test for the SNP before he'll let them play with the Smith Commission on further devolution. He's helpfully provided only one option for the tick box, which is helpfully labelled 'wrong answer'. Wullie thinks this is a cunning ruse and he's set a very clever trap. Awwwww. Someone give him a smartie.

The test consists of a vow, there's a lot of those going around just now. People must catch them in lifts, like Yes voters with a cold and other viruses of nationalism. The SNP have got to vow not to tell the Smith Commission they want an unstable form of devolution that will only lead to independence. Wullie doesn't actually know what an unstable form of devolution is, seeing as how no one is very sure what a stable variety would look like, but he does know that unstable will be what the Lib Dems call absolutely any proposal put forward by the SNP.

Meanwhile the Koalamichael is getting agitated about another referendum, and wants the SNP to rule it out forever. Because if the people of Scotland are not told once and for all that they can never change their minds ever, not even if circumstances change, then it will be just like Quebec where they keep having new referendums. Then Edinburgh will turn into Montreal and this will be very bad for the banks because all the ATMs will be in French. The thrust of the argument being that the self-interest of the finance industry is more important than silly little things like democracy, or vows not being kept by balloons.

And this pretty much sums up the attitude of the Westminster parties, whether it's the Blue Tories, the Red Tories, the Purple Raving Nigel Fan Club Tories, or the Yellow Greasy Enabling Tories - all of them believe that it's only the populace which should be held to any sort of commitment, never their own party. All that's left for us is to be lectured by a garden gnome and a stuffed toy koala on an entitlement kick.

Let's kick them out.

Oh God, Why Did I Ever Think This Was a Good Idea?

10 October 2014

I'm now at the "oh God why did I ever think this was a good idea" stage in the house flitting process, and am sitting here surrounded by packing cases and piles of assorted stuff all over the floor, under which - somewhere - is hiding a roll of parcel tape. It's hiding on purpose, because it's malevolent. The guy in Gordon's Supplies, Lies and Trussing shop where I bought it swore blind that it was really good and would do exactly what I wanted, so it was only my own fault for believing a vow. You see when someone tells you it's a done deal, it means you've been done.

So what with arguing with recalcitrant packing tape, choosing wallpaper, spending hours on the phone to the electricity company, and packing stuff away - I've not really been keeping abreast of political developments of late or had much time to update the blog. But you don't need to pay close attention to realise just how much trouble all three of the main Westminster parties are in. It's a bit like watching an overhyped boxer fighting to the death with a plastic spatula, and the spatula is winning.

The simultaneous descent of all three main parties into disrepute is quite a remarkable achievement in a First Past the Post electoral system where distaste for one party generally results in strengthening one of the others. But that's just how rubbish our current crop of party leaders are - they've even broken a political system that was designed so that one or other of them would be in power for perpetuity, with or without the occasional Lib Dem dangleberry - they cling on so persistently. And it's all the more remarkable when you consider that this is a system that was set up to cope with chinless wonders with stiff upper lips who never needed a spoon because they were already born with silver ones preinstalled in their gobs.

The Lib Dem conference was still going on for most of the week, although no one noticed. I think it was still going on yesterday, but like 99.99% of the population I couldn't be bothered to find out. The remaining 0.01% is related to a Lib Dem MP and hears about it whether they like it or not. Usually not.

Meanwhile the realisation is dawning within the upper reaches of the British Labour hierarchy that in Ed Miliband they really did pick a plasticine Wallace as party leader but Ed Balls comes nowhere close to Grommit the dog in competence or likeability. With opinion poll ratings showing that Labour has thrown away its previous lead in the polls, it's looking highly unlikely that the party will become the largest party in the next parliament, never mind the government.

The Tories on the other hand had a "good" conference. "Good" in this instance being defined as tearing up the European Human Rights treaty, tax cuts for the better off, putting a great big English votes for English laws fly in the devolution jam, and sawing off the legs of people on benefits so that golf club members in Surrey can run them down in a golf cart. This has made the Tories more popular with people who have Death Race 2000 on DVD and aspire to the membership of golf clubs in Surrey.

However the Tory feel good bounce, achieved by using a disabled person as a springboard, has been splattered due to a by-election in the previously Tory seat of Clacton which fell to UKIP and give the purple faced right wing populists their first directly elected MP. Douglas Carswell won with an embarrassingly large 60% of all votes cast. It was one of the biggest swings to any party since in decades. Nigel Farage, who permanently wears the smug expression of a late developer who has just discovered masturbation and thinks he's got a special secret no one else knows, is going to have to buy in a bulk order of paper towels from the cash and carry.

Tory rumblings of discontent with Davie's leadership were already rumbling before Clacton. Now the pressure on the Tories to tack even further to the right is going to be intense, and we can expect a lot more in the way of "fairness for England" as an excuse to delay Scottish devolution, and hyping up the anti-Europe rhetoric.

Labour's woes have also taken on a deep purplish hue. The other by-election on Thursday was in the Heywood and Middleton constituency in Manchester. It was supposedly a safe Labour seat, as recently as 2001 Labour took 57.7% of all votes cast. But UKIP came within a tickle of making Nigel have to go and get a new supply of tissues again, and reduced Labour's majority to just

617. A whole swathe of Labour seats in England suddenly became as vulnerable as a baw hair in a Brazilian waxing salon. There's those plastic spatulas again. Turn-out was a pathetically low 36%. There's no apathy like British Labour engendered apathy. It's one of the few things they're very good at.

Although Labour held on to the seat, in some ways the result in Heywood was worse for them. In Clacton Douglas Carswell was the sitting MP before he switched to UKIP. He was, apparently, popular locally. I know. Go figure. No I don't get it either, but there ye go. He had an established presence in the seat. Like one of those dents on your favourite chair that's shaped itself into the perfect shape of your bum. In Clacton Carswell was the right arse. But in Heywood UKIP came from nowhere, and almost succeeded in planking their arse very firmly on a sofa that Labour has always thought it was its divine right to get on expenses from John Lewis.

Meanwhile in Scotland, British Labour is in a whole different set of bother. Those of you who voted Yes can go "muwahahahaha" at this juncture, like an evil supervillain. Go on, you know you want to. I've been practising my special "told you so" smug look.

The Lib Dems avoided humiliation, but only by securing the sole rights to ignominy, disgrace, and mortification. And made a strong bid for ridicule too, but were only saved by there being so much ridicule to go around these days. In Clacton they managed a paltry 483 votes, and a lost deposit of £500. They would have been better off bribing 483 voters a quid each and then they'd still have had enough left over for a curry.

UKIP have now proven that they can take votes from both Labour and the Tories, and the Lib Dems have been consigned to oblivion. They've done this because of rather than despite of the fact that they have no policies besides getting out of Europe, kicking Scotland, and hating immigrants. They're the party for people who hate politicians, but who don't have any real consensus yet on what they want to do about it.

That's where Scotland is way ahead of the game. There is a whole ferment of ideas and new projects amongst the 45. Scotland is slowly reaching towards a new consensus on how this country should be governed, and who it should be governed for. They look to what's happening down south, and many of those who voted No are now having "oh God why did I ever think this was a good idea" moments of their own.

We're in for some very choppy waters along the way, but the current weak and discredited condition of the parties and institutions of the UK means that an organised mass movement can gain huge concessions. And we've had a two year long education in organising ourselves.

Newton's Law of Y-Fronts

14 October 2014

When I'm not wondering why I have a waffle iron, and am still unclear on what a waffle iron is, never mind wondering why there's one in the cupboard, I've been on the phone to utilities companies, insurance agents, and the rest of the practicalities required for a flitting. But the big day is looming, the removal van will appear at the door one week from today, and there's still so much to do. Oh God. Panic. Panic. This is why you're not getting so many blog posts of late, looking after a dementia sufferer was almost relaxing by comparison.

I'm drowning under a sea of packing cases, books, and a vast quantity of detritus that people sell on eBay as 'collectables', like a cracked old candle in the shape of Bugs Bunny dressed as Carmen Miranda that was given as a birthday present over 30 years ago and which will never be lit, it was much more recently joined by a stuffed toy Wee Ginger Dug made by a reader of this blog. However neither Bugs nor the wee dug will ever be sold on eBay. And probably neither will most of the rest of the crap that's currently littering the living room carpet. It's going to follow me around for the rest of my life like a stray dog that looks at you with big brown eyes and makes you feel guilty. He's still following me around too, and is at this very moment giving one of his special accusatory stares, the kind he reserves for when he wants you to know that he's not been out for a few hours

... Right, the dug has been walked now ...

So, election debates, pure dead exciting innit. We can all shout at the telly that we don't agree with Nick, and rather feel like taking Nick by the scruff of the neck and setting his pants on fire. In fact many of us want to do that with all of them. It would certainly make debates more interesting, and quicker, as party leaders rushed to explain their policies on taxation before the flames removed the last of their pubic hair. Although I don't think anyone as shiny as Davie Cameron has any.

For the correct degree of gravitas with the gravy train arses, the programme should be presented by Dale Winton, who can ask the contestants, sorry - political leaders - for their opinions on the latest war in Iraq and whether they believe that Ermintrude from the Magic Roundabout was a right cow after she left Zebedee in the lurch at the altar and ran off with Dylan to get stoned in a hippy commune near Brighton.

Dale can emote in a dayglo orange while a clock ticks and the contestants will be tipped backwards into a big pool of goo if they get the answer wrong. The eventual winner gets to take home the key to Number 10, a new motor, unlimited foreign trips staying in the best hotels, and will become besties with the presenter of Top Gear - except Ed Miliband, who'll get a dinner date with that guy with the teeth who used to be on Big Brother, or was it the X-Factor. Then Ed can learn from a master of being famous for being famous while having no appreciable talent at all. Ben Fogle wasn't available.

All this would at least make the programme interesting for Scottish viewers, because our full range of democratic choices won't be only display. The SNP and the Greens are not going to be invited to the debate, because they're not important. Scotland isn't important either, a proposition with which 55% of the country agreed last month, at least according to the broadcasters, so they don't have to take us into account when deciding who's going to get gooey with Dale. SNP voters can see a wee cute kitten stuck in a drain in Falkirk on Reporting Scotland instead, or if you're a Green voter there may be a beardy folk singer on BBC Alba explaining renewable energy policy through the medium of jigs and reels.

Only the leaders of parties which could actually form the government of the UK are going to be invited to participate in the main debate. So that's us telt then. The SNP are a mere provincial regional county parish party, and don't even put up candidates in important places - which is anywhere within a 20 mile radius of the M25 in case you were wondering. That's why Dale won't deign to goo them. So naturally Davie Cameron and Ed Miliband get to come along, and Nick's got to come too because he's their governmental vaseline.

And Nigel needs to come along as well, because he's got an MP now and it is entirely possible that large numbers of people in important places will consider voting for him and he could be swept into power, like it's entirely possible that the atoms making up Nigel's body could spontaneously rearrange themselves into a candle in the shape of Bugs Bunny dressed as Carmen Miranda. I'd set light to that one, so Nigel could drip all over Dale's shag pile and melt away to nothing.

Fair enough, although the spontaneous rearrangement of Nigel Farage's atoms is possible, for a given value of possible, it is vanishingly improbable, but there is a law of physics that says that exact thing can happen, Newton's fifth law of incendiary Y-fronts. You can't say that for the SNP. This is all detailed in the BBC's top secret election debate manual, just after the chapter where it explains that the BBC is Nigel's publicity agent and is contractually obliged to have him on the telly every day. He's on Bargain Hunt all this week, looking for 1950's social attitudes at a car boot sale in Colchester. Tim thinks it's a bit orff.

None of this means that the spontaneous rearrangement of constituent parts is always improbable, since it's already happened. I seem to recall that just a few short weeks ago, before a certain vote, Scotland was being told it was a much valued partner in the bestest union of nations in the universe ever, but now the UK has rearranged its constituent parts and we're back in an over-centralised unitary state again. We must be, because it's only in a centralised unitary state that major political parties representing one part of what some of us thought was supposed to be a union can be legitimately excluded from a UK election debate. Or perhaps I just misunderstood Gordie, like he apparently misunderstood Davie, Nick and Ed when they vowed to him it was a done deal about all that devosuperpowermax federalism stuff. Although it's considerably more probable than the spontaneous rearrangement of constituent parts that Gordie just made it all up to suit himself, just like the BBC's debate rules.

How Now Brown's Vow

18 October 2014

The road to Hell, blog posts, and post-referendum vows is paved with good intentions. Or at least that holds true for two items on the list, whether there were ever any good intentions in the vow is very much a matter for debate. In fact, it's debatable whether there ever was a vow in the first place, because it is not beyond the bounds of possibility that it only ever existed in the febrile minds of Gordie and the editor of the Daily Record. More a ciao than a vow then, as it meant we could say goodbye to any hopes of substantive extra powers for Holyrood.

In the Peanuts cartoon strip, there was a recurring gag when Charlie Brown attempted to kick a football, one of those oddly shaped ones like Gordie's heid, held into place by his friend Lucy. Whenever Charlie Brown went to kick the baw, Lucy wheeched it away. Yet Charlie Brown fell for it every time. He's clearly a close relative of Gordie. Lucy was never going to let Charlie Brown kick the baw, just like Westminster was never going to fulfil the vow that Gordie assured us was a done deal. Snoopy won't be doing his happy dance.

The debates in Westminster this week were ostensibly about extra powers for Scotland and the implementation of the infamous vow, however the debate was taken up almost in its entirety with arguments over English devolution. Predictably, proceedings descended into Labour and the Tories arguing over what was best for their own party interests. The only person who seemed shocked by this turn of events was Charlie, sorry, Gordie. This is because if anyone is going to break their word but pretend that they haven't, it will be Gordie, and he's not happy that others have trodden on astroturf he regards as rightfully his.

Despite his much heralded intellect, Gordie suffers from a very special kind of stupid, the kind that only highly intelligent and deeply vain people suffer from, people whose IQs are the square root of their egos. Gordie may be highly intelligent in getting a PhD about the early history of the Labour party, but he has the social intelligence of monkey wrench. He is, quite literally, a tool. People like Gordie get used by those who may not partake in his impressively large ego, his intellectualosity, and his ability to come out with phrases like endogenous growth devolution, but who are far more politically and socially shrewd. Lenin called monkey wrenches like Gordie 'useful idiots'. Gordie was played, brought down by his own ego and the mistaken belief that he can out-think everyone around him. It's the arrogance of the small town boy who was always the brightest in his class at school, and who thinks this means he's brighter than everyone on the planet.

If I was ever a telly interviewer, there's a question I'd like to put to Gordie - I'd ask him to name one, just one, policy he had implemented because it was the right thing to do, even though it had damaged his party's chances of election and his own career. Bet ye he couldn't answer, and this is why I'll never be a telly interviewer - I wouldn't let it go. Gordie has never willingly put the greater good above the interests of Gordie and the British Labour party, because in Gordie's eye the greater good always, by an eerie coincidence, just happens to be what's good for Gordie. Spooky.

Yet this is the same Gordie who wanted voters to believe that he, and the rest of the misbegotten Westminster party leaders, would put aside personal and party interests in order to fulfil a vow to the people of Scotland. And Gordie, being the tool fool that he is, probably genuinely believed that Davie, Ed and Nick would go along with what was good for Gordie. Davie Cameron looked at Gordie's proposal for a vow, and saw a monkey wrench to stick in the devo-works. It is below the belt to cast aspersions on a person's mental health - but you do have to wonder whether Gordie is just a bit of a nutter. Actually no. You don't need to wonder, it's really quite certain that Gordie's contact with reality is at best tangential.

On Friday Gordie published an article in the Guardian. The focus of his upset was not what happens to Scotland under Cameron's proposals for devolution, but rather what happens to Scottish MPs. Or more specifically, to him and his British Labour co-conspirators. They will no longer be able to vote on "English only" matters. And by devolving all income tax, Cameron has ensured that's going to include the budget. At a stroke, Gordie, the Smurph and St Dougie the Creeping Jesus will be denied the possibility of cabinet seats. That's the second classness that really bothers Gordie, not the second class nature of a hauf airsed devolution proposal that includes a random selection of tax raising powers but doesn't include much else, and certainly not the ability for Holyrood to set up a Scottish national TV channel.

Gordie doesn't need to worry, because there may not be that many second class British Labour MPs in Scotland after the next General Election. They're all third class runners up, and there won't be that many of them. The latest polls show that British Labour is about to experience its very own version of lemmingdom. Since the referendum the party's vote share in Scotland has fallen off a cliff. In the most recent YouGov poll, the Scottish subsample shows that British Labour is - almost unbelievably - returning a lower vote share than the Tories. The Tories poll 20%, British Labour a paltry 19%. "Others", those small parties and regional parochial parties too insignificant for YouGov to notice, have been polling over 50%. That'll be the SNP and the Greens then. Although other polls do show Labour ahead of the Tories in Scotland - although not by much - all agree that the SNP and the other pro-independence parties are well ahead, and UKIP, the BBC's favourite "other party" is nowhere to be seen.

The BBC is doing all it can to rescue the situation, and has decided quite arbitrarily that the SNP, the Greens, and Plaid Cymru will be excluded from the leaders' debates scheduled for before the next General Election. It's all that stands between business as usual and the prospect that pro-independence MPs will hold a majority of Scottish Westminster seats. That will mean that Westminster's devolution proposals will be unlikely to secure a democratic mandate within Scotland, and will instead have to be imposed by English votes. English Votes for Scottish Laws, it was ever thus.

Magrit Curran better hurry up with her consultation of pissed off East Enders then. The only thing I don't like about my new hoose is that Magrit is my MP - although probably only until May. The seat fell to the SNP in the 2008 by-election.

I'm still waiting for my invite to yer consultation Magrit, by the way. I'd be delighted to tell you at length and in colourful detail exactly where things have gone wrong for you, and why it's far too late for you to do anything about it. All that's left for Magrit is to consult under a rock along with Wullie Bain and Ian Davidson.

Many years ago I remarked that Scotland would become independent, not because it was the expressed and settled will of the voters of Scotland, but because the Westminster parties would be incapable of putting the continuation of the Union above narrow party interests. That's one prediction that looks like coming true. If only I had the same success with lottery numbers.

There will not be any more blog posts this week. The big flitting is on Tuesday, and I am currently surrounded by packing cases and I won't have internet access until everything is reconnected in the new house. And I'm trying to give up smoking. With limited success, so I am really, really tetchy right now. Magrit, you have been warned.

A Wee Update About Flitting and Fags

October 23 2014

The fact I'm posting this ought to let you know that I'm back online again - whoo hoo. But this isn't a post about the Smith Commission, the British Labour party, or any wit and wisdom about anything remotely political. It's just a wee update to let you know what's going on with the big flit.

The move went smoothly, and we managed to get everything over to the new flat without breaking anything. Although my uncle did point out a loose wire on a model train when he was looking at it. Every single time that man looks at a model train or tram, it gets broken. It's not even his fault either. He hadn't even touched the train. He's just cursed. He is to model trains as Gordie Broon is to politics, come to think of it. Although in Broon's case it generally is his fault. And you can't fix the devolution settlement with a bit of solder, you'll only get burned.

I'm now unpacking everything, and working my way through all the packing cases. I've got loads of lovely things that haven't seen the light of day since we moved back from Spain. And a shitload of crap too. Mostly crap. I'm still wondering why I have a waffle iron.

I've not had a fag since 2.30am on Tuesday morning, when I finished the last of the baccy I'd found in a tin in a drawer in the old place. On Saturday while suffering a severe craving I distracted myself by clearing out rubbish - only to discover a wee bit of rolling tobacco hiding there. So that was the giving up smoking buggered for last weekend. Until I finished that very last little bit. I've not used nicotine patches, e-cigs, or thon boggin tasting chewing gum, I've just gone cold turkey - and to my surprise it's working. And I'm not even eating lots of sweeties.

I don't want to smoke in this new flat - and haven't. Moving has made it easier to give up because I've changed my routine. I still sit and watch Pointless with a cuppa, just not with a fag any more. I'm watching it in a different house in a different place - and it feels sufficiently different that the craving for the ciggie is controllable. I am determined to do it this time.

I'm still getting cravings of course, but they're bearable. When I was a teenager I used to bite my fingernails, but managed to stop that by playing with a wee lump of plasticine instead. Believe it or not I still have the original lump of plasticine - which is now a solid ball bearing very little resemblance to modelling clay. But it fits my hands perfectly, and when I get a craving for a ciggy I roll the ball between my hands. Fingers crossed it's working, or rather I would cross my fingers but they're occupied with a ball of plasticine.

I have no idea what's going on in the news - but I'll try and catch up with myself and all going well normal posting service will be resumed over the weekend.

Is Schadenfreude Fatal?

25 October 2014

Less than two months since Scotland voted No, and it's become clear that the big loser from the independence referendum isn't the SNP or the other pro-independence parties, it's Labour. Is schadenfreude fatal? I may have given up ciggies just to die from an overdose of smugness, gloating, and an overwhelming urge to yell out: "Ha ha! Fuckin' TELT yese!"

Johann Lamont famously told Scots that we are not genetically programmed to make decisions, but now she herself has been programmed - a bit like a washing machine - and has decided to leave Labour to its rinse and spin cycle. The woman who has spent the last two years telling us that being ruled from London like a branch office is a good thing has resigned as leader of British Labour in Scotland - because the party in Scotland is being run from London like a branch office. No, really, pick your jaw up off the floor.

There's some serious irony lurking there. Well, not so much lurking as standing in front of you in a day-glo spandex irony suit screaming "Look at me I'm the dictionary definition of irony, you bastard" into your face. It's irony that's so unsubtle that even Alanis

Morrisette would pick up on it for a song lyric. Johann can't spot it though. Johann doesn't do irony, or indeed intellectual coherence, joined up thinking, or sentences with a subject, a verb, and an object. Actually it transcends irony, iron is a base metal. What we see before us in the British Labour party is something heavier, rarer and far more toxic, it's plutoniumy. They're entirely artificial, radioactive, destructive of all that is organic, and have a limited half-life. It couldn't have happened to a more deserving bunch of self-serving careerists.

What Johann does do is lobbing a few grenades in the direction of Labour's Scottish MPs and Ed Miliband. Or as he's known in the Lamont household - that fucking useless skinny wanker. The Labour MPs are, according to Johann, dinosaurs - a discovery that Johann has only recently made. The rest of us realised this long before the asteroid that wiped them out crashed into the Yucatan peninsula where it created a massive crater known as Chicxulub, which is Yucatec Maya for "Jim Murphy's expenses". So vast, it can be seen from outer space.

However, the reports in the media that Johann has resigned as leader of Scottish Labour are not strictly true. There is no such party as Scottish Labour - Scottish Labour is a branding exercise belonging to the British Labour party and has no distinct existence of its own. A non-party can't have a leader, and indeed Johann was very much the model of a non-leader, non-leaders all over the world looked to her for inspiration on how not to lead. It is more accurate to say that Johann was the fictitious leader of a fictitious party who has fictitiously resigned.

When Johann was elected as the fictitious leader of a fictitious party, British Labour swore a vow that she would be a proper non-leader, and would non-lead Westminster MPs as well as Holyrood MSPs and local cooncillors. It was of course a deception. But Johann took the gig and was quite happy to go along with the deception right up to the point where she realised that she was one of those who was being deceived.

Johann's resignation was allegedly provoked in part by the discovery that Magrit Curran - her auld pal fae uni and co-conspirator - was canvassing members of the party's ruling executive in order to get them to persuade Johann to resign. Magrit and Johann go back a long way together, but personal loyalty counts for about as much as a manifesto promise or a referendum vow in the Labour party. Magrit Curran - the wummin that's too venal for tribalism. But the straw that broke the humphy camel's back came when Labour's leadership in London decided to sack Ian Price, the general secretary of the Labour party in Scotland, without anyone consulting Johann, which is a bit like giving someone a house then breaking in and redecorating the living room with puce green flock wallpaper without telling them.

Today the Guardian is reporting that for over a year Johann was forbidden from criticising the bedroom tax - a key issue in the referendum campaign - until Ed Miliband had made up his mind on the issue. This is code for "consulted with focus groups of voters in key English marginals". Labour's policy is set, as it has always been set, by the need to persuade Tory, and now UKIP, leaning voters in marginal constituencies to vote Labour. There are no such seats in Scotland, so the demands of Scotland's electorate simply do not figure in British Labour's calculations. We get to be taken for granted - and now Johann has found out that getting taken for granted is a bit of a pisser, so she's voted with her feet. There's all Magrit Curran needs to know for her wee commission investigating why Labour is about as appealing as a centrifuge full of dysentery victims.

The question now is who is going to accept the poisoned chalice and take over as leader of the moribund bunch of expenses claimants, time-servers, arselickers and greasy pole climbers. The range of potential candidates is less than inspiring. Some in Labour are pushing for Gordie Broon, the recently declared Saviour of the Nation, however his political career is hanging by a vow. Jim Murphy's name has been mentioned, by people who don't spit while saying it, which is something of a novelty for Jim. But that would be an effective demotion for a man who has spent his political career fighting to advance a sacred principle which can be summed up in just two words - those words being "Jim" and "Murphy". Plus he's a warmongering Blairite whose past will most assuredly follow him like the smell of a bad egg. Kezia Dugdale, of all people, has been mentioned, and you know things are desperate when Kezia is regarded as a plus, but she didn't get the BBC radio show so she needs something to do with herself.

Still, you can console yourselves with the thought that no one has mentioned Jackie Baillie as a new possible leader, but that's only because - judging by her performance on Good Morning Scotland on Saturday - she has finally taken leave of what little senses she once possessed.

So that just leaves the hereditary MP for Govan, the millionaire slimebucket otherwise known as Anas Sarwar, who as deputy has taken over as fictitious interim leader of the fictitious Scottish Labour party. This is perfectly appropriate, seeing as how Anas is a fictitious human being. But he has no intention of giving up the Westminster seat bequeathed to him by daddy - it's a family heirloom after all.

Meanwhile the UK polls show that Labour is slipping behind a Tory party which is itself riven with infighting and division, and in Scotland the SNP surges ahead in Westminster voting intentions. Looks like we're going to find out whether schadenfreude is fatal, but Labour's condition certainly is.

Still not had a ciggy - that's almost 5 days now. Dear God I could murder for a fag. But I am resisting temptation. Explains a lot about why I'm so venomous about the Labour party in Scotland.

Spermatozoa and Jim Murphy

27 October 2014

What happens when you call an election and no one comes? Labour looks like it may be about to find out as each of those tipped as future pretendy leader of the pretendy "Scottish Labour" branch office rule themselves out the running. It's like a PE fitba selection in reverse - oh dear God don't pick me. None of the dinosaurs want the job because they're staring extinction in the face as it is, and besides, Ian Davidson has issued a statement saying he's got to stay in and wash his hair. None of the so-called big hitters want the job because they know they'll only get hit bigger. None of the young hopefuls want the job because they would like to have a career that lasts longer than a tub of lard held up to a hair dryer. At the rate things are going, we'd end up with Jackie Baillie because there's no one else left. However Jackie has also ruled herself out, on account of the fact that she'd melt.

On Monday Gordie Broon announced doesn't want the job because it would mean he'd actually have to do some work and attend sessions of Parliament - and then stand for Holyrood and attend there. It would have a serious impact on his career as an after dinner spokes hypnotist, helping businesspersons who can't switch off to enjoy a good sleep. Gordie has an aversion to being challenged, so he can't stand as it would mean that he'd be challenged weekly at FMQs. He didn't spend the entire referendum campaign talking to no one but hand-picked audiences for nothing. Hand-picked audiences of Labour supporters don't answer back.

Anas Sarwar, the interim hereditary leader, announced today that he won't stand as his daddy won't let him give up the family heirloom seat in Govan. Holding the seat in Govan is sort of like being the Prince of Wales, it's occupied by the future Governor of the Punjab. Anas has fond hopes that one day he can pass it on to his own wee Sarwar, who - according to a persistent rumour -Anas sends to a private school because he doesn't want his children to associate with the kind of scruff that Anas relies on to vote for him.

Anas refusing to stand means that there is a very real likelihood that both the leader and deputy leader of the ahem "Scottish" Labour party will be Westminster MPs - an eventuality which rather proves Johann's branch office run from London point. Jim Murphy is the only well known name who has not so far ruled himself out. Jim thinks he'd be a great leader because he fancies himself as spunky. Like a spermatozoa, Jim has a one in a billion chance of turning into a real human being. Many in the party think that Jim is ideal for the job as he epitomises all that the moribund modern Labour party stands for - self-serving careerism, bloated expenses claims, a dictatorial nature, a willful failure to listen to or understand what Scottish voters want, a complete lack of principles, and as a bonus he already looks like a cadaver.

58

The other potential contender is a guy called Neil Findlay, a list MSP for Lothian whose main selling point is that no one outside of Holyrood's Labour group has ever heard of him, and half of Holyrood's Labour group haven't heard of him either. This is a major advantage as it makes Neil one of the very few Labour politicians in Scotland who don't provoke guffaws and derisory howls from the electorate whenever their name is mentioned, although I'm sure that won't last long. Neil wants to take Labour to the left, and recover the party's socialist principles, hoping to appeal to that aged and dying off section of the voting public which can actually remember when Labour was supposed to be a left wing party. Which is no one under the age of 90.

The problem with Neil's prospectus is of course that even if he does succeed in taking the pretendy leadership of a party the doesn't really exist, the dinosaurs in charge of the branch office will put the kybosh on his leftwards movement in about as long as it takes to say velociraptor. It may be relevant at this juncture to point out that the makers of the Jurassic Park movie took considerable liberties in the depiction of the velociraptor, which in real life was about the size of a turkey. This would make Labour the first organisation in the history of politics to have been culled by an extinct turkey. And it's not even Christmas.

There's been some speculation in the media, or at least by Alex Massie, that Jim Murphy represents the only serious threat to the SNP and this is why he's attracted the most attacks from 45ers on social media. This is not true. The reason Jim Murphy is a favourite target of attacks is because he's Jim Murphy. Why bother attacking someone no one has ever heard of when you can launch a few verbal lobs at the man who sums up in a single individual all that has gone wrong with Labour over the past 20 odd years. What's the problem with Labour? Jim Murphy. See - that makes sense.

But a new leader - whether it's the death-head Jim or the guy nobody knows - won't be able to solve Labour's problems. Today we've had a succession of Labour figures on the telly telling us that Johann was quite mistaken when she said that they were out of touch, and proved it by denying that there were any issues to address at all. David Blunkett was aghast at the very notion that Labour in Scotland might have policies that differ from those of Labour elsewhere in the UK, demonstrating that he hasn't quite grasped the concept of "Scottish Labour" as anything other than a brand name for Ed Miliband north of the border. This is as much a problem for Labour as Jim Murphy is.

Meanwhile the Smith Commission is working to a strict timetable as Labour tears itself apart. Does anyone know any more what Labour is proposing for our lovely new devolution settlement? Did anyone know before Johann resigned? Answers on a postcard to the Smith Commission.

Red Pandas and Pop Tarts

31 October 2014

The red panda is a real thing. It's much smaller beastie than the better known giant panda, but it's only marginally less endangered. According to Wikipedia, the red panda faces extinction because of habitat fragmentation, inbreeding, and poaching - which by a happy set of coincidences also form the reasons why the red pandas of the Labour party in Scotland are also staring extinction in the face. No one is really sure what sort of creature a red panda is, but it looks like some sort of weasel, a bit like Ian Davidson with a full head of ginger hair. Real red pandas are much cuter than Jim Murphy however, but then so is a snake in the grass slithering through dog mess.

Red pandadom beckons after STV published an IPSOS Mori opinion poll of voting intentions in next year's Westminster revenge match - when the voters on Scotland get to boot the Westminster political parties in the glands as punishment for being a bunch of self-serving self-regarding self-abusers. The poll, fieldwork for which was carried out as Johann Lamont resigned as branch office manager, shows that the SNP stand to receive a whopping 52% of votes in Scotland. The SNP enjoy a lead of 29% over Labour - meaning that the SNP's lead is greater than Labour's entire vote share of 23%.

Translated into seats, Labour would be left with just four MPs in Scotland, which makes the red pandas marginally less endangered than the giant pandas of the Tory party - just like the real pandas. Spooky, and just in time for Halloween.

The poor polling news was compounded by another poll from YouGov which was only marginally less desperate for Labour. Like the desperation difference between wanting to throw yourself off a cliff, and wanting to throw yourself off a cliff after you've slit your wrists. If translated into seats, YouGov's poll would give Labour just ten useless bench occupiers.

Despite the dire polling figures, Labour isn't toast. Toast is home-made and often organic. Labour is a pop tart, chock full of artificial ingredients which appeals only to those with no political taste buds. Labour is likewise filled with a red coloured goo which bears the same relationship to socialism as the contents of a pop tart do to real fruit. And the Labour leadership's favourite Gordon Ramsay stand-in who will rescue this culinary disaster zone while swearing a lot is apparently Jim Murphy - a right wing, ultra-Blairite, Iraq war supporting, expenses junky, egg magnet.

Jim promises that if he's elected as branch manager, he will stop Labour in Scotland from self-harming and will put an end to its obsessional in-fighting. And this is true, because it's Jim and his pals who've been engaging in most of the self-harming and obsessional in-fighting by briefing against Johann and anyone else that Jim thinks stands between him and his career plans.

I did have to laugh though, when Jim said that the Labour party needed to find some passion again. Jim and the rest of the sorry careerists who pride themselves on "professional" politics are precisely those who have leeched anything resembling passion from politics, with their focus groups and triangulation. There is however plenty of passion in Scottish politics - it's just a pity for Labour that it's the passion of those who are intent on bringing about the long overdue demise of a Labour party that's become a parody of its former self, a party that's as progressive as a pop tart with imaginary jam.

Labour is now facing another election - it's going to have to elect a new deputy branch manager following the resignation of Anas Sarwar. Anas has resigned in order to remove the inevitable objection to Jim Murphy's election which would have led to both the branch manager and the deputy branch manager being Westminster MPs. Anas is an obedient little Labour placeperson, he does what his daddy tells him, and he does what Jim Murphy tells him too.

Anas's resignation as deputy manager of Scotmid conveniently delays the need for Jim to find a safe Holyrood seat. This is very handy for two reasons. Firstly because there's no such thing as a safe Labour seat at Holyrood any more, and secondly - as pointed out by Lallands Peat Worrier - the plan mooted by some senior party figures for a Labour MSP who plans to retire in 2016 to be persuaded to stand down a year earlier is a non-starter because it would mean that he or she would lose their pension rights. And it would force an election purely for reasons internal to Labour, a situation which the voting public is unlikely to look kindly upon, all the more so when they are already looking on Labour as kindly as an axe wielding maniac who's just given up smoking. Over ten days now - in case you're wondering. But I've never knowingly wielded an axe. Just a sharp tongue.

The root cause of this seismic shift in Labour's Westminster electoral prospects is that Scotland's voters have finally decided that the well-established tactic of differential voting in Holyrood and Westminster elections is an idea whose time is past. There is no point in voting Labour in Westminster elections in order to keep the Tories out for a number of reasons - not the least of which being that Labour stood shoulder to shoulder with the Tories throughout the referendum campaign. And if there is little chance that Labour can win the election in England, then there is absolutely no point at all voting Labour in Scotland in order to protect ourselves from Tory governments. We're going to get the Tories anyway, whether that's yer actual Tory basterts, or a Labour party that apes Tory policies in order to sook up to Tory leaning voters in English marginal constituencies.

It's not that Scottish tactical voting is dead - it's just that it's got a whole lot smarter. There's nothing Labour can do to turn things around, you can't turn around a sinking ship. The only question remaining is the scale of their defeat. Labour's tea is oot - they're being served burned pop tarts and red pandas.

Jim Murphy's BOGOF

2 November 2014

Less than two months after the referendum, you know, that vote that was supposed to establish the settled will of the Scottish people until the Sun expands in a ball of hot gas and consumes the Earth - or at least for the length of the career of the average Labour politician - a new poll from YouGov has discovered that a significant number of No voters have changed their minds and now want independence. The other significant development is that two months is now also about the average career life of a Labour politician in Scotland. Only may flies have a shorter life expectancy, but they don't have any mouth parts. Sadly the same cannot be said for Jim Murphy. A male may fly is basically nothing more than a mobile reproductive organ - it's just a dick sniffing for something to screw - which you can indeed say for Jim Murphy, so order is restored to the universe.

Despite the oft repeated media message that the candidate most feared by "the nationalists" is Jim Murphy - a message largely put about by Jim Murphy and his supporters - it's not. It's Sarah Boyack. She is the only candidate with any chance at all of uniting the ragged remains of British Labour in Scotland, and putting an end to its knee-jerk circle-jerk. It's not a big chance. It is a tiny wee chance, but it's a chance nonetheless. Jim has nae chance. All Jim is capable of uniting is his bank balance and an expenses claim, or a Middle Eastern country and a Western invasion.

In the interests of full disclosure, I should point out that I knew Sarah Boyack at university - she was a Labour hack even then, and a protege of Magrit Curran and Johann. People can and do change, all those years ago I had a whole lot more hair and a head that was very firmly lodged up my own arse, but Sarah is still a Labour hack. Even so, on a personal level she's a decent human being. She is also the only one of the three candidates who does not automatically respond to all and any proposal from the SNP as though it was contaminated with the ebola virus. And this is why Sarah has no chance of getting elected.

Even Neil Findlay would make a better party branch manager than Jim. Neil's idea of taking Labour back to the left is essentially the correct one - but it has precisely zero chance of ever being implemented. Westminster Labour is not going to permit its Scottish branch office to introduce left wing policies which would make it unelectable in England, and the Scottish electorate is not going to be fooled by a Labour party which preaches one thing in Scotland and something else in the rest of the UK. We get the English news on Scottish telly, thanks to the Unionists' parties insistence that broadcasting is a reserved matter.

Not that either Sarah or Neil have much chance of success even if one of them were elected branch office manager. The truth is that even if British Labour possessed a candidate with the political guile of Machiavelli, the moral stature of Mahatma Gandhi, and the intelligence of Albert Einstein - the party would still be screwed. It's far too late now, and a change of leadership isn't nearly enough to turn Labour's fortunes around. Labour in Scotland has been a long time dying, but it finally shuffled off into an irretrievable demise the day that Davie Cameron persuaded ASDA's managing director to issue a scare about price rises after independence, and Johann and her wee bunch of minions stood outside a branch of the supermarket grinning like skulls. There is absolutely nothing left for Labour except to crawl under a rock and rot away, unmourned, and unloved, not even fit for the cut price shelf for items at their sell by date.

There's now a full on media onslaught pushing the Smurph. Sarah Boyack and the other guy - the Ken MacIntosh of this branch manager campaign - have been side-lined and ignored. Other guy is likely to pick up some trade union support in the Byzantine system of elections used by Labour for its branch managers, but the party hierarchy has put its weight very firmly behind the Smugurph. Ed Miliband is very keen for him to get the job, because he hates Jim Murphy as much as anyone else and he's hoping that the Smugurph will condescend his way to Embra and conveniently remove himself from Westminster. Ed views Jim candidacy as a sort of supermarket BOGOF offer. He gets rid of a troublesome plotter who hates him, and at the same time gets a "big hitter" to rescue his arse in Scotland - or so he thinks.

Mostly he just wants Jim to BOGOF, a sentiment he shares with pretty much everyone else. Labour are the baked beans of politics, and just as likely to make you fart.

Meanwhile the Smugurph's chances of being anything other than a long distance branch manager are receding faster than Ed Miliband's chances of becoming the next prime minister. Ed may very well end up with the worst of all possible outcomes - he'll have the odious Jim as Scottish branch manager, and Jim will still be in Westminster. At least until May next year. The Sunday Herald reports today that the three MSPs whose names have been suggested - by Jim's pals, it has to be said - as willing to stand down in order to allow Jim to contest their seats in a by-election held on the same day as the Westminster General Election have all said that they intend to remain in Holyrood. So nae chance for Jim there then.

This gives Jim a big problem. If he can't find a seat in Holyrood before the 2016 Scottish elections when he can sneak in as a list MSP, he'll have to contest his Westminster seat in May 2015. This is because Labour's rules state quite clearly that their Scottish branch manager has to be either an MP, an MSP or an MEP. And with the current mood of the Scottish electorate, it's by no means certain that Jim would retain his seat in East Renfrewshire. If he fails to be re-elected, he'd have to stand down as party branch manager and it would be an ignominious end to a less than glorious career as well as an end to his expenses claims. You can be certain that the SNP and the other pro-independence parties will be doing all they can to ensure that Jim gets his jotters in May.

Up in Smoke

6 November 2014

I t's only after you break a bad habit that you realise just how bad it was for you. Like giving up smoking or voting Labour in Scotland. That's been a vicious addiction that hundreds of thousands have given up, and which they have no intention of returning to - it's been much easier than giving up smoking. Labour produces nasty bile and shortens your life span. Vote Labour and get cancer of the body politic.

That's now over two weeks without a ciggie and I'm feeling increasingly confident that this time I've given up for good. From time to time I still think about how much I'd love a smoke, but the cravings are not strong and far less frequent than they used to be. I don't ever think that I'd love to vote Labour, I never wistfully wonder what it would be like to have a wee sly drag on Jim Murphy just for old time's sake. But Ed Miliband wants us to sook on Jim Murphy so he doesn't have to. It's a very easy temptation to resist, like the temptation to lick a turd or the temptation to have a wet dream about Ed Miliband.

Labour's appalling polling figures continue to plunge to new depths. A poll for STV this week shows that they'd do even worse in a Holyrood election than the unprecedented thrashing they got in 2011. The poll

70

showed that they'd get just 23% of the vote share, well down from the 31.7% they managed in 2011. By an eerie coincidence, 23% is also the proportion of Scottish adults who still smoke - and that's falling too, although not quite as quickly as Labour's vote share. Labour's the fag-end party, the only thing left about it are doubts and a lingering smell. Their prospects of re-election have gone up in smoke.

Labour is increasingly resembling a Cheech and Chong movie, 1980s comedies beloved of those who are too stoned to notice that the jokes are rubbish and the plot about hash is rehashed. If that's not enough to drive you to drugs then probably nothing is. This is why the party organ is the Daily Record, with its reading age of seven. Labour has the concentration span of a goldfish on speed. The party would have to study for a week for a urine test, and they'd still fail. Now they want us to believe that reality is an illusion caused by a lack of Jim Murphy and Kezia Dugdale, this is because Labour is a gateway drug - that explains how it's ended up in Narnia. However there is an essential difference between people who get stoned on a regular basis and Labour politicians. Labour politicians don't inhale, they just suck.

What didn't go up in smoke was an effigy of Alicsammin in Lewes in Sussex, in the heart of Toryukip Ingerland, as opposed to Lewis in the Western Isles. One of these places is barren, far from civilisation and inhabited by narrow minded bigots with 19th century attitudes, the other is an island off the West Coast of Scotland. Or maybe the effigy did go up in smoke, reports on the subject have been as confused as Labour's attempts to

71

find some coherent policies. Some people on Twitter and social media were claiming that at least one of the effigies was burned after all. Anyway, Lewes is somewhere that few in Scotland had heard about and even fewer cared about right up to the point where we heard that they were going to set fire to a papier maché effigy of Alicsammin and Nessie as part of their Guy Fawkes celebrations. Because burning Catholics just isn't offensive enough.

It's all just a bit of fun of course, and only humourless nats get offended by this sort of thing. I have no particular objection to burning an effigy of Alicsammin - it's just a tasteless tradition which the non-PC residents of a town I've never visited and am never likely to visit indulge themselves in each year. They're previously burned effigies of Angela Merkel and other European politicians as well as effigies of Cameron and Clegg. It's a tradition not unlike the Catalan tradition of caganers, when every Christmas they exhibit an effigy of a public figure dropping a jobby. It's supposed to be 'naughty', and to provoke a giggle in the likes of people who go to golf clubs in Sussex and vote UKIP. It's a joke for the kind of people who think Jim Davidson is funny. And to be fair, those of us who voted Yes do want to bring down the Westminster Parliament - even though it's in an entirely peaceful and democratic manner. We are modern Guy Fawkeses. We certainly put a rocket up the arse of the British establishment during the referendum campaign.

What is interesting however is the non-reciprocal nature of the humour. It's always just a bit of harmless fun when the English indulge in offensive stereotyping of

Scottish people. It's not a bit of harmless fun when Scottish people indulge in offensive stereotyping of English people, because this points to something dark and evyle lurking at the very heart of the Scottish psyche. There is a persistent English racist stereotype that the sole definitive feature of Scottish culture is a hatred of English people. Being Scottish is all about the English, apparently. So it's not the burning of an effigy of Alicsammin that annoys me. It's the double standards. We saw it all the way through the referendum campaign, from Steve Bell's cartoons to the hysterical editorials bewailing the anti-English racism that is supposed to stalk every street in Scotland.

Imagining the reaction if Scottish people burned an effigy of David Cameron isn't quite a reasonable comparison, because if Yes voters had made a Guy Fawkes night effigy of Cameron, half the voters of England would have come to Scotland with matches - in fact half the Conservative party would have supplied cans of petrol and napalm. Instead - imagine the reaction from the anti-independence parties if Yes voters had burned effigies of Alistair Darling, Gordie Broon, and Jim Murphy. Would anyone be telling us then that it was just a joke and where's yer sense of humour? The polis would have been called before anyone could say egg-flinger.

So the response from outraged Scots isn't really about burning an effigy of Alicsammin - or even an effigy of Nessie - what's outraging them is the fact that others are being indulged in behaviours which they can't do in response. It's the non-reciprocal nature of what is considered "harmless fun". That's what's unfair, that's what's offensive, not the effigy of Alicsammin.

I Want My Devo-Max

9 November 2014

So where's my devo max then? Like most people in Scotland who have been following political developments over the past few years - which is most people in Scotland - I fancy I have quite a good idea of what the phrase "devo max" means. It means that the Scottish Parliament raises all its own revenue including oil revenues, and exercises all powers except those to do with foreign affairs and defence - which would be retained by the UK Parliament. Seems straightforward enough doesn't it. There would be no arguments about supposed "subsidies" from England, no disagreements over Scottish MPs voting on English only matters. What's not to like? And as the icing on the devo cake, this is the settlement which, according to opinion polls, is consistently favoured by a large majority of the Scottish population, and had it been on offer prior to the independence referendum campaign, there wouldn't have been an independence referendum campaign.

I seem to recall that during a certain referendum campaign a certain ex-prime minister promised us the most maxiest devo you could ever find this side of a federal state. In fact, we were promised the most federalest devo maxiest in the history of this most perfect union of nations ever seen in the history of the multiverse. It was all over the BBC, which as we all know is famous for its realistic depiction of all things Scottish - just watch Waterloo Road for its realistic depiction of a school that follows the English curriculum even though it's in Greenock. Point proven.

Onieweys, this promise - or dare I say vow - came when yer actual prime minister and the heads of the other Unionist parties were all quite happy for the ex-prime minister to act like he was still prime minister, although to be fair Gordie Broon's relationship with his employment status has always erred on the side of fictional. This is after all the man who described himself as an ex-politician while he's still the MP for Kirkcaldy and who can rarely be arsed to turn up to represent them in the House of Commons.

What we were promised by Gordie and his tangential relationship to reality was for Holyrood and the other devolved administrations in the UK to have "the same status" as the Westminster Parliament. The new sort of federal government, according to the ex-politician ex-prime minister, would retain powers over defence and foreign affairs - everything else would be left to the control of the national parliaments. Gordie's promise was going to save the UK, and that's what Gordie's promise did. Only Gordie's promise was never going to be realised and it has now gone much the same way as the Labour party's prospects of re-election in Scotland. There's more chance of reviving a velociraptor for Jurassic park than there is of resuscitating devo max - or the Labour party.

Just a few days before the vote, Gordie vowed:

"The status quo is no longer an option. The choice is now between irreversible separation, or voting for a stronger Scottish parliament. We are talking about a big change in the constitution. It's like home rule in the UK. We would be moving quite close to something near to federalism in a country where 85 per cent of the population is from one nation. Change is in the air and change is coming."

Two months after the event and it doesn't look like the Unionist parties are going to deliver anything close to that. Gordie himself stood up in Westminster and laid into the Tories because they wanted to devolve more taxes than he did. That's the Tories, offering more devo than Labour - the self-described "party of devolution". And then Labour wonders why its polling ratings have plunged further than a jobby that's been flushed from a tenth floor toilet.

Still, Unionist politicians don't have to keep their words, because Unionist politicians' words mean whatever the Unionist politician wants them to mean at any given moment. Gordie might be an ex-politician, but he's not an ex-fantasist. The devo max Gordie promised bears a similar relationship to reality as his promise to end boom and bust. That's devo max bust then. As are the Unionist parties.

Devo max is not on offer after all, not even close. The Unionist parties are proposing some minor tinkering with the existing settlement, arguing about what percentage of income tax revenues can dance on the head of a Holyrood pin. It's devo-get-what-you're-given, devo-dae-as-yer-telt. It's the devolution that suits the political requirements of the Labour, Tory and Lib Dem front benches.

Devo max will never be offered by the Unionist parties for one very simple reason - it stands the relationship between Holyrood and Westminster on its head. Under the current devolution settlement, powers devolved are powers retained - and the ultimate power rests very firmly with Westminster. It means that they can preserve the fiction that only the Westminster Parliament is sovereign - and not the Scottish people. So Westminster collects all the taxes, and decides how much Holyrood is going to get. In the process it is conveniently able to obscure just how much of a contribution Scotland and Scottish resources make towards the extremely expensive upkeep of the United Kingdom and its addiction to nuclear missiles, foreign wars, and transport infrastructure in the South East of England. Then when Scotland gets uppity they can threaten us with warnings of financial meltdown without the kindness of Davie Cameron and Ed Miliband to look out for us.

With proper devo max, that couldn't happen. Proper devo max means that Westminster's fiction of the sovereignty of parliament is rendered meaningless and toothless. Holyrood would be responsible for raising all Scottish revenues, so Westminster would no longer be able to cook the books and tell us we were dependent upon them. And Holyrood would no longer be dependent upon a block grant from Westminster, it would be the other way around - Westminster would receive a grant from Holyrood to pay for those services which remained under centralised UK control - defence and foreign affairs. In effect this gives Holyrood a veto over Westminster's foreign adventures - should there be another Iraq, then the Scottish Parliament might just refuse to pay its annual subvention to Westminster to pay for Scotland's share of the costs of an illegal war. That's why the Westminster parties won't allow devo max, no matter how popular it is with the Scottish electorate, and no matter how often or loudly we demand it of them.

So if you want something that is yours by right, but the other party is not disposed to give it, then all that is left is to take it. We can do that by ensuring that at the next Westminster General Election and the next Scottish elections we return a majority of pro-Scotland MPs who can block any attempts by Westminster to impose a devolution settlement which falls short of the devo max they promised. It's up to us to ensure they keep their promises, and to punish them if they try - as they most assuredly will - to weasel out of it.

The On-coming Train

13 November 2014

According to the Herald, Jim Murphy has promised that if he wins the election for manager of Labour's Scottish dead meat counter he's going to wrest power back from the London office. What he really means of course is that he'll take what powers he can for himself, because this is Jim Murphy we're talking about here. Whispering Jim's ego is inversely proportional to the loudness of his voice. Jim Murphy has a vision for Scotland's future, it's a picture of him towering about his tiny little minions - the murphoids. Murphoids are small and narrow minded things that cling to Labour like haemorrhoids, only bloodless and drained of anything red. He fancies himself as a supervillain, but he's sadly bereft of any superpowers, except the powers to schmooze with interviewers on the BBC, and the power to turn socialist policies into Tory ones.

Demoted from his defence brief in the shadow cabinet after the Brownite faction won the succession struggle and Jim had hitched his horse whispering to Tony Blair's pony, the Smugurphy's London career has gone the way of Ed Miliband's re-election prospects, side-lined and forgotten like mention of the deficit in Ed's keynote conference speech. The answer to what Jim sees as the greatest political crisis so far this century - the crisis of his own career vanishing more quickly than Magrit Curran being faced with an irate East End voter - is to build himself a new power base in Scotland. He's done this because he still suffers from the delusion that the Labour party has a power base left in Scotland.

Jim's move does raise some interesting questions which he has shown no sign of answering and Andrew whitsisface with the prematurely white hair on the BBC's excuse for a Scottish politics and news show showed no sign of asking. But that's what happens when you have to work for Ken McQuarrie - you age unnaturally quickly. People born in the 1970s end up looking like they're channelling the 1950s, which is where the BBC's concept of news and current affairs in Scotland has remained stuck like a knob on a black and white telly. Or just a knob.

Anyway, there was a review of Labour policy and procedure carried out after the last time the Scottish electorate kicked the empty suits of Labour in the balls, or rather, kicked them where their balls would be if they possessed any balls in the first place. This was a review carried out by Jim Murphy and Sarah Boyack, both of whom are now standing for election as branch office manager. The review set up the office of Leader of Scottish Labour (sic - and sick was rarely more appropriate), and gave us the delights of the lovely Johann Lamont and her radiant smile. We were told at the time that the new leader would have all those powers that Jim Murphy now tells us he's going to wrest from Labour's London office.

So how come Jim Murphy is the guy to sort the problems in the Labour party in Scotland, when it was the failure of Jim Murphy's own review that led to the problems that Labour is currently experiencing? Was this review of Jim's not implemented then? If not, why not, and who is responsible for not implementing it?

No one is asking Jim. Probably because Jim is one of those responsible for not implementing it. Jim never had any intention of allowing a Scottish branch of Labour to have any control at all. He's only interested in the control he wields himself, and that's why he's spent the past six months briefing furiously against Johann and then sanctimoniously saying that the party must stop damaging itself. He's one of the dinosaurs that Johann complained about in her bitter resignation letter. Getting the Smugurph in to sort the party out is like suffering a brain haemorrhage and deciding to treat it by slashing your wrists and leaping in front of an oncoming train.

The train is coming - there's no light at the end of Labour's tunnel, it's the train. The Caledonian Express is going to plaster the Labour party's electoral hopes in Scotland all over the tracks like the jam they always promised but never delivered. The train is powered by lies and deceit. It's driven by the engine of deception, the promises that the Clyde yards would only be safe if Scotland voted No, promises delivered amidst po-faced assertions that the Royal Navy would never commission ships from a foreign land. And now the post-referendum reality where the MoD has admitted that it is considering pulling the Clyde contracts and buying French ships instead. The head of angry steam is building. It's going to explode in a shower of votes in May next year.

A new UK wide poll from IPSOS Mori has shown that the SNP is on 8% - that's 8% across the entire UK - just 1% behind the UK polling figure for the Lib Dems. There's some serious rounding issues going on there, because the SNP only stand in Scotland and Scotland makes up just 8.5% of the UK electorate. A more detailed breakdown of the figures shows that in Scotland, the SNP has the support of 59% of voters against - wait for it - just 14% who back the murphoids. That would annihilate Labour in Scotland, and not even the blindly loyal Labour voters of Coatbridge would be left to them. If this latest poll is accurate - and it's not wildly out of line with recent Scotland only polls - the SNP could easily become the third largest party in the next Westminster Parliament. Now that would be a laff. The SNP could hold the balance of power in the next Westminster Parliament. We might just get that devo max after all.

But what the polls do show is that without any doubt or quibbles about rounding, or the small sizes of Scottish subsample, or any of the other get-out clauses usually trotted out at these times - Labour in Scotland is gubbed. More gubbed than a gobstopper that's evaded the Heimlich manoeuvre. Now you know why the party appears Tory blue in the face. Choke on that one Jim. Your career is about to hit the buffers. The party leader with no party to lead.

Portillo Moments on Steroids

18 November 2014

So that's it then, the end of an era. Alicsammin has bowed out as leader of the SNP. But it's not the last we'll be seeing of him, he's going to be a thorn in the flesh of the Westminster parties for quite some time to come. Alicsammin is the marmite of Scottish politics, loved and loathed in equal measure, but no one can deny that he's changed Scotland forever. This is not the same country that it was back in 2007 when the SNP narrowly pipped Labour at the post and became the minority government, putting an end to what was supposed to be the permanent Labour-Lib Dem duopoly set up in a back room meeting between Donald Dewer and Ming Campbell.

Back then Labour thought it was just a wee blip and normal service would be resumed just as soon as the rest of Scotland realised what a terrible mistake they'd made by rejecting the self-described peepil's party. All Labour had to do was sit back, sling mud, and the voters would return to their 'natural home'. The mud was duly slung, and has been slung repeatedly and regularly ever since. Mud-slinging has been Labour's substitute for politics. Labour didn't think it needed to change, after all it was the voters who'd made the mistake. They're the people's party, and they decide what's right for the people, never that the people decide and a real people's party follows. It was the arrogance of those who accuse others of arrogance, and it bit them in the bum. However such is the size of Labour's complacent lardarse that seven years later the lesson is still chewing its way through. It still hasn't reached the Anas.

And Alicsammin laughed and ran rings around them as Labour squirmed and couldn't understand why there was an uncomfortable itch that anusol couldn't relieve. Even though the battle of the referendum was lost, the wider campaign for independence is buoyant. Alicsammin's greatest achievement wasn't to bring about the referendum. His greatest achievement has been to normalise the idea of independence. That's the truly historic change that has taken place in Scotland under the government led by Alex Salmond - he's shown us that Scotland can be a normal country, all we have to do is to believe in ourselves. And many of us already do.

Now a few short months after the referendum was won by the forces of Nawness, we are in a landscape that is alien and frightening to the Westminster hegemonists. Labour is still squirming and still can't understand what's gone wrong. They cry for reviews, they promise commissions, they suggest they want debates. But really all they want is for everything to go back to the way it was before that nasty Alicsammin changed everything. The electorate has left them behind and Labour is left clutching an empty bottle of Buckie at a party no one wants to attend.

It wasn't supposed to be like this. No won the referendum, Yes supporters were supposed to crawl away and hide under a rock in the vain hope that they might avoid Ian Davidson's bayonet. But instead it's Ian Davidson and his pals who are wounded and looking at the sharp end of a bayonet. They're bleeding bad - in both senses of the phrase.

So Alicsammin hasn't sailed off into the sunset, under a cloud, doomed to an ignominious retirement overshadowed by his great failure. Instead he's off to open a new front and twist that bayonet some more. He's after a seat in Westminster where he can be a permanent bayonet in Ian Davidson's quivering flesh - assuming that Ian Davidson is one of those Labour MPs who survive the culling that will befall them in May 2015. The prospects for most of them don't look good at all. Yet another poll has shown Labour's chances of avoiding an electoral armageddon are vanishing more quickly than Ed Miliband's fond regards for Johann Lamont.

A new Survation poll for the Record puts Labour on a derisory 23.9%, with the SNP on 45.8%. The new poll is in line with previous recent polls, and the SNP is now gaining the level of support which will make the first past the post system work in its favour. There are no safe Labour seats in Scotland any more. Glasgow East is certainly not safe for Magrit Curran - it's where I live and I'll be doing my utmost to ensure that Magrit gets her jotters. All across Scotland other angry Yes voters will be working equally hard to rewrite the Proclaimers song lyrics. When ye go, will ye send back a cheque for your expenses. Magrit no more, Tom Harris no more, Dougie no more, Smugurphy no more ... There will be Portillo moments on steroids.

There is a distinct possibility that pro-Scotland MPs may be the third largest force in the Westminster parliament after May 2015. There's an equally distinct possibility that the Lib Dems in Scotland may be reduced to just Alistair Carmichael all on his tod. Commentators in England view this possibility with horror - not the possibility that the Lib Dems might get wiped out, everyone with a sense of justice who can remember their solemn vow on student fees relishes that prospect - the prospect that a bloc of MPs who put Scotland's interests first might hold the balance of power is what they view with horror. And there was us thinking that Scotland had voted No so we were all a part of this happy family of nations. But apparently it's only a happy family when Scotland does as Scotland is told.

There are those south of the border who fear that the dominance of the SNP and other pro-Scotland parties north of the border means that pro-Scotland MPs could hold the balance of power at Westminster after May 2015. Some have expressed alarm that this could mean that England might get screwed over by Scotland. They needn't worry. England will get screwed over by England, like it has always been. These pro-Scotland MPs, who would be largely SNP MPs, might prop up a Labour government even if Labour gained fewer Westminster seats in England than the Tories do. The notion that England might not get the government it votes for is terrifying - there's only one response anyone from north of the border can make to that: welcome to Scotland's world.

Back from London

26 November 2014

So I go away for a few days, and have a great time apart from a rampant allergy to my daughters' cats, and all sorts of things happen in my absence. Gordon Brown announces that he's standing down at the next election, UKIP kicks both the Tories and Labour up the backside in a by-election in Rochester, Niclasturjun replaces Alicsammin as the synonym for Scottish independence in the British media and holds a rally attended by thoosands, the Radical Independence Campaign hold a conference just over the road also attended by thoosands, many of whom are the same thoosands as those who went to see Nicola, a new pro-independence newspaper gets launched without a regular column by a small reddish canine who's really quite affordable (cough cough), and Jim Murphy had a damascene conversion and discovered some real political principles. OK, so that last bit is a lie.

Let's start with Gordie, whose departure from politics was announced to the general surprise of everyone who thought he'd already departed. But Gordie's toddling off into a sunset of devoting himself to extremely well remunerated soporific after dinner speeches does raise an interesting question, one which is unlikely to be answered by Gordon Brown. Nor indeed asked by an extremely well remunerated BBC politics correspondent who didn't get the job because they're related to John Smith.

Mind you, Gordon doesn't answer questions, and certainly not questions posed by anyone who hasn't been vetted beforehand. But for what it's worth the question in question is: Was it not Gordon who swore blind that he personally would ensure that the Vow with the Capital Letters would be implemented by the Westminster Parliament after the May 2015 election? This was when he was still pretending he was the current as opposed to the former Prime Minister, and the current as opposed to the soon to be former Prime Minister was quite happy for him to do so.

The answer would appear to be that Gordie can just as easily ensure the passage of the Vow by not attending Parliament as a former MP as he can by not attending Parliament as the MP for Kirkcaldy. So that's sorted then, and the Scottish electorate must be terribly reassured. Or, which is more likely, past the point of caring about anything Gordie says or does.

Dahn sarf, UKIP won the by-election in Rochester in the latest episode in the English electorate's miserabilist challenge to the entrenched Westminster parties. Funny isn't it, it's supposed to be Scots who are dour and miserable, yet our challenge to Westminster's business as usual is relentlessly cheerful, upbeat, and outward looking. Meanwhile in England many people complain that they have no one to vote for since the only realistic challengers to the existing system are a bunch of neo-

Thatcherites who want to retreat into some imagined golden age of the 1950s which never existed. So if you live in England and hate Westminster, you can vote for UKIP, a party which promises to increase the powers of Westminster. That's a deeply unattractive proposition even before you look at the grinning self-satisfied mug of Nigel Bawbag Farage.

But the truth - a truth which the UK media is unlikely to dwell on - is that after the next Westminster elections UKIP are unlikely to gain more than a handful of seats. The first past the post system of voting, which UKIP favour, pretty much guarantees the continuation of the existing duopoly unless a party can establish itself as the largest single force in a constituency. Then the first past the post system works in that party's favour. And this is why Nicola is so buoyant, because the SNP looks like it's made that breakthrough in Scotland. She's also ensured gender equality in the Scottish cabinet, making Scotland one of the best performing countries in the world in terms of women's representation in politics - although there's certainly still a long way to go. Westminster, in case you were wondering, is way down the rankings, bobbing along somewhere in the 1950s where women made the tea for Nigel Farage. Westminster only talks about increasing female representation in politics, Scotland does something about it. Mind you, only just over a quarter of SNP MSPs are women, so Nicola's still got her work cut out for her.

A series of opinion polls have shown that the SNP is well in the lead in Westminster voting intention, and may very well reduce Labour to a small rump despite the best efforts of the BBC to marginalise distinctively Scottish voices. The SNP continue to pile on new members, while Labour's membership figures in Scotland remain a closely guarded secret. While the SNP is on course to have 100,000 members by the time of the Westminster General Election, Labour in all probability has fewer than a tenth of that number. These are the folk who'll be chapping on doors, delivering leaflets and getting the vote out, and in Labour's supposedly safe seats in the Yes voting areas of the Central Belt, they're outnumbered over 10 to one by the SNP. And that's before you start counting the Greens, SSP, and unaffiliated Radical Independence supporters, who have likewise piled on new members - all of whom will be just as eager to ensure that Labour gets a kicking for wrapping itself in the Union flag and standing shoulder to shoulder with the Tories.

Aware that his party is more screwed than a lightbulb in a joke factory, Jim Murphy has announced that he may, or may not, be in favour of devolving control of all income tax to Holyrood after all. This is a considered policy decision which is the exact opposite of his considered policy decision last week when devolving income tax would be the worst thing to happen to Scotland since the bubonic plague. But enough about Ian Davidson. Of course the real reason for the announcement is to get Jim in the papers, and to try to rescue Labour from being the party offering the weakest devolution proposals - weaker even than the Tories. It also, handily, gives Jim a stick with which to beat the SNP, as he can promise to increase taxes on the richest. Jim claims this will raise £250 million a year in entirely made up statistics. The real figure is a tiny fraction of that, but what's accuracy when you're a Labour politician? It's only SNP politicians that the BBC holds to account, so that's OK then.

Jim can make these announcements and get them plastered all over the telly and the papers because the telly and the papers have decided that he's already the branch manager of the Labour party's unstocked supermarket in Scotland. Jim's in charge of the checkouts, and he and his party will be checking out very soon. The other contenders for branch manager have been relegated to the stock cupboard, where they're currently fully occupied with counting the number of members the party has lost over the past few years.

It's pretty obvious to one and all that the Labour leadership - the only Labour leadership which counts, the one in London - has already decided that Whispering Jim Smugurphy will get the gig as branch manager. It suits Ed Miliband to get rid of a troublesome Blairite, Ed would rather Jim was fully occupied in Scotland than engaging in briefing campaigns against his shoogly peg of a leadership. Jim is quite happy to take over in Scotland, because he sees it as the last chance he's got of rescuing his ailing career, and we all know by now, Jim Murphy's career progression constitutes the nearest thing to a set of principles that Jim Murphy has got.

And finally - apropos of nothing in particular. That's over a month now without a ciggy, and I think I can finally call myself an ex-smoker.

Eyewash and Plastic Spades

28 November 2014

You've been promised something revolutionary and ground-breaking which is going to change the way you look at the world. This very special present has been placed in a huge box wrapped up in pretty paper specially printed by the Daily Record, and put under a Christmas tree with a devolution fairy on top, if you're good little boys and girls Gordie Broon is going to wave his magic vowing wand for you. Finally, to a fanfare from the BBC and a chorus of MPs, you're allowed to open the enormous container, and discover that it contains a three-way air freshener - the whiffs of Tory disdain, Lib Dem duplicity and Labour desperation - a plastic toy spade, and a small bottle of Optrex.

So that's the Smith Commission then. Home rule it isn't, as despite what the UK media and the Westminster parties might tell you there is no definition of 'home rule' which doesn't include having control of the TV remote. You might want to watch something else, but you'll have to sit through the Strictly Come Westminster Debate Show whether you like it or not and get to watch David Cameron and Ed Miliband's pirouette in ever decreasing circles while Nigel Farage in an attention grabbing tutu tries to steal the show. Nicola wasn't invited to take part, since she's not enough of a celeb.

There was no mention of broadcasting in the Smith Commission report, Scotland's home rule doesn't extend as far as allowing us to decide on our own broadcasting regulation - or, heaven forfend - giving the Scottish Parliament the authority to set up a Scottish national publicly owned TV channel. There was no mention of a lot of other things either, instead we got a whole lot of waffle without any substance - tax powers which will not allow Scotland to raise any more revenue than Westminster wants us to. Scotland can raise rate of income tax on the highest earners, only to see the UK Treasury reduce the block grant correspondingly. Westminster has played this trick before, the Smith Commission is merely a repeat performance. It's the devolution of austerity, not the devolution of substantive powers that might allow Scotland to determine a different course.

The proposals were watered down even before the final report was written. Labour insisted that control over abortion law couldn't possibly be devolved, on the entirely spurious grounds that this would mean the end of a UK-wide abortion policy. No one has told them about Northern Ireland then. The reason for Labour's refusal was one time SNP funder Brian Souter, who is apparently the only person in Scotland who gets to decide such matters. Like he was so influential in determining the SNP and Scottish Government policy on banning gay marriage ...

The promised powers over welfare and benefits policy were also gutted like a fish even before a kipper got anywhere near them. Proposals to allow Holyrood to determine the benefits system in Scotland were removed at the insistence of Satan, otherwise known as Iain Duncan Smith, who was upset that his policy of damning benefits claimants to perdition for all eternity might be smited. In the end, Holyrood will only have control of limited powers over Housing Benefit.

The real significance of the Smith Commission isn't what it means for devolution, it's what it means for the future of the UK. Many years ago I remarked to a friend that Scotland would not become independent because it was the settled will of the Scottish people, but rather independence would arrive because of the short termism and political games of the Westminster parties who would be unable to find a formula to keep the UK together. With the Smith Commission, the break-up of the UK took a great leap forward. For that reason, and for that reason alone, the Smith Commission is to be welcomed.

Davie Cameron has already announced that the taxation responsibilities in the report give him licence to introduce a bill for 'English votes for English laws'. Scottish MPs are to be barred from voting on certain parts of the UK budget, in a nakedly political manoeuvre to screw over the Labour party. It's a trap that Labour walked straight into, one from which they now have no escape. That's what happens when Alistair Darling accepts the cheers of a Tory party conference, Labour MPs accept Tory donations, and Labour MSPs stand grinning outside supermarkets after a Tory MP has phoned the managing director to get him to issue a press release warning of price rises after independence.

Labour is now reaping what it sowed, and even if it does manage to cling onto a significant number of Scottish seats after the May 2015 General Election, their MPs will be castrated. Not that any of them have ever had much in the way of balls to begin with. It couldn't happen to a more deserving bunch of hypocritical Pharisees.

Alistair Koalamichael was reduced to pleading that "this is the Prime Minister's view, not government policy", conveniently forgetting that under the system of elective dictatorship which passes for democracy in the UK, the prime minister's view is government policy. Poor wee Alistair doesn't even understand the system of government he's pledged himself to defend. So we can add that to the very long list of things that Alistair doesn't understand, like irony, impending oblivion, and keeping manifesto promises.

But despite the hype, despite the screaming headlines, the Smith Commission report is just that, a report from a commission. There is no guarantee that the recommendations in the report will survive the labyrinths of the Palace of Westminster, inhabited by ancient monsters which devour devolution maidens. Scotland must now rely upon the parties which have spent the past two years arguing that there is no need for extra tax powers for Holyrood to implement these extra tax powers - or rather tax responsibilities. We saw the same with the Calman Commission, which recommended the devolution of airport duty only for the proposal to land nowhere near its advertised destination. The Smith Commission is a dodgy budget airline all over again, complete with hidden costs.

Want to get to Devo Max? You'll get dumped miles away. You should have got on the independence bus. But don't worry if you missed the bus, there will be another along very soon.

Resetting Gordie Broon

1 December 2014

Gordie Broon doesn't want Scotland to obsess about constitutional change. In this instance we can be certain that Scotland's very own political Walter Mitty knows what he's talking about because if you obsess over things you turn into Gordie Broon. He's worried because it looks like the voters of Scotland are going to throw a metaphorical Nokia at the Labour party and hold a grudge against them until they're hounded out of office forever left with nothing but a reputation for crimes against humanity and a clutch of cushy directorships, somewhat like he did with Tony Blair.

In a speech at the weekend to a hand-picked audience of the dwindling band of Labour loyalists - because Gordie only speaks to folk who have been vetted and who sign an agreement not to jeer - Gordie said he wanted to press the reset button on Scottish politics and the constitution. The speech was conveniently splattered all over the BBC news so that the rest of us didn't miss it, those of us who haven't been vetted and are quite likely to jeer because we've heard this sort of guff from Gordie before.

Gordie's announced he's resigning as an MP, which is only making it official as he's rarely been bothered enough about the concerns of the good people of Kirkcaldy to turn up at Westminster to represent them. But his resignation does mean that when the Smith Commission and Gordie's vow crash and burn, Gordie won't be there to cop the flak. He'll be off mumbling about endogenous growth theory - which is apparently something to do with warts - on the highly lucrative corporate speechifying circuit. But at least it does mean that the voters of Kirkcaldy get the opportunity to press the reset button on their MP, and might even get one who can be arsed enough to do some work.

Pressing the reset button on Scottish politics and constitutional wrangling is entirely appropriate as reset is a good Scots word, referring to the crime of holding something which was taken by theft or by a breach of trust such as fraud or wilful imposition - you know, like Labour and the other Unionist parties have done with the sovereignty of the Scottish people in the pathetic excuse for more devolution delivered by the Smith Commission. Glad you've cleared that up for us then Gordie. Can we call the polis now?

The Smith Commission report has been dissected and digested by everyone in Scotland with at least a passing interest in politics - which is a most of the electorate - and the general consensus of opinion amongst everyone who isn't a Unionist politician, a wannabe Unionist politician, or an editorialist in most of the media, is "Well that's a bit rubbish then, isn't it." The Smith Commission gives us the absolute minimum which the Unionists think can be fobbed off as fulfilling Gordie's Vow - the one which promised as close to federalism as it was possible to get and full home rule.

The problem for the Unionists however is that a politically literate electorate is unlikely to be fooled by their scrawlings in crayon all over the constitutional settlement. Although to be fair, we don't have a constitutional settlement so much as we have a constitutional campsite, complete with discarded bin bags full of devolution proposals that never got through Commons committees, and an old caravan which Labour MPs use for weekend piss ups. But the latest addition - the Smith Commission BBQ and Grill - is not going to toast the aspirations of the majority of Scottish voters who want devo max. Scottish voters know what home rule means, they know what devo max means. The Smith Commission doesn't come remotely close.

Yesterday the Sunday Herald reported on the many and varied powers which had originally been considered as part of the Smith Commission proposals, but which were filleted at the insistence of one or other of the self-described parties of devolution. Labour, the Tories, and the Lib Dems spent most of their negotiating time on the phone to headquarters in London and then demanding that various powers were removed from the final report.

Labour - shamefully - demanded the removal of powers over the minimum wage. Labour would have us believe that a Westminster Parliament dominated by Conservatives and looking forward to an ever increasing number of Thatcherite UKIP MPs is going to be a better defender of the rights of the low paid than a Scottish

Parliament dominated by MSPs from parties from social democratic parties. The only reason that Labour did this is its tribal hatred of the SNP.

The same goes for the removal from the Smith report of powers over the abortion law. Labour opposed devolution of this - apparently citing the spurious reason that it would mean there would no longer be a single cut-off date for abortions throughout the UK. There never has been, as Northern Ireland was exempt from the original abortion law and abortion remains illegal in the province. But Labour refuses to cede powers to Holyrood simply because it hates the SNP so much. What's in the interests of the people of Scotland don't figure in Labour's considerations at all. It's the very definition of holding the voters in contempt.

But it may all be academic anyway. It needs to be stressed, repeated, and screamed from the rooftops that the Smith Commission's proposals are merely proposals. We've been here before with the Calman Commission. New powers over this that and the other were announced to great fanfare, we were told that this was the devolution settlement that would finally put the issue to bed for a generation or more and Scotland could hit the reset button and get back to normal politics instead of constant constitutional wrangling. As we all know, that's not what happened. We got devo-hee-haw instead.

Many of the Calman Commission's proposals were removed in Commons Committees - powers which have once again surfaced as proposals in the Smith

Commission. There's no guarantee that Unionist parties which were dead set against these powers the last time are any more disposed to allow them through the Commons this time. Quite the reverse, this time Westminster is far more interested in limiting the power and influence of Scotland, or more precisely, Labour MPs representing Scottish seats, and that in turn will only hasten the day that the dysfunctional UK comes shuddering to its final unlamented demise. That will be Gordie's real lasting legacy.

Wullie Rennie's Letter to Santa

4 December 2014

Just three months after the referendum, and for much of the Scottish political class and their media hingers oan it's back to business as usual. This consists of finding things to accuse the SNP of while displaying a moral outrage that a hormonal teenager who's just painted their bedroom black and retired under the duvet would consider a bit immature. And then they wonder why the public hold politicians and the media in contempt.

This week we've had two invitations to throw our hands in the air in horror and purse our lips like a Wee Free who's stumbled into a Gay Pride march in Stornoway on a Sunday. There may have been more SNP accused moments, but on Monday and Tuesday BBC Scotland and the Record were far too busy trying to persuade us that Gordie Broon was really one of the X-men - a superhero who's the offspring of Mother Theresa and Gandhi with the intellect of Einstein - and I'd been overcome with projectile vomiting and had to go and lie down in a darkened room so didn't notice. Gordie's superhero persona is endogenous growth man - which is a bit like a verucca but with added Nokia hurling, bullying, and behind the scenes briefings. Gordie's politics were an ingrowing wart on the sole of socialism.

Anyway, first up was Wullie Rennie, attempting to be noticed again. Wullie has to pull moronic stunts on regular basis as otherwise the rest of the world would forget he exists as something other than a character from a Dudley D Watkins cartoon - one of those who's been badly drawn after the great man had popped his clogs. That, and the fact that Lib Dems have been staring extinction in the face for longer than a diplodocus, only far less nifty on their feet.

This week Wullie's wheeze was to reveal to a shocked Lib Dem pamphlet, one channelling a Wee Free at a Gay Pride March in Stornoway, that Scottish Government civil servants have been looking at evil nationalist websites. It's the curse of Wings again, flying high over Scotland, and dumping guano on the Unionist establishment.

Looking at Wings Over Scotland is a bad bad thing, because civil servants must never allow their eyes to be polluted with biased sources, except those like poorly sub-edited Lib Dem pamphlets or the Aberdeen Press and Journal. But it's not bias when it agrees with Wullie. The Unionist parties, the Unionist media, and a number of pro-independence supporters who really ought to have known better spent much of the referendum campaign portraying Stu Campbell, the author of Wings Over Scotland, as a sort of cross between a cult leader and a J Edgar Hoover without the taste for cross dressing.

Ooh that Stu Campbell is a homophobic monster, heterosexual people cried in unison, because he'd had a number of inconsequential twitter spats with inconsequential people and said some things they hoped that other people might find objectionable. It is of course a well-known rule of Scottish politics that only people who are saint-like in their dispositions are allowed to make any contribution to political discourse - so that would be saints like Gordie Broon then, former employer of Damien McBride, Iraq war enabler, and the man who condemned a generation to low paid employment subsidised by those of us who can't avoid paying our taxes while allowing the banks to run riot and selling off state assets. But Gordon's never said anything objectionable on Twitter, so that makes everything else he's ever said or done perfectly OK.

The real reason for the stunt was of course to provide the tame press with an excuse to accuse Nicola Sturgeon of something. Cue newspaper articles demanding that the new First Minister disassociate herself from a website she's not associated with and has no control over anyway. Next week Nicola will be called upon to disassociate herself from North Korean pirate downloaders, a guy on Twitter who pretends to be Philip Schofield, two serial shaggers on the Jeremy Kyle Show, and a spotty child in a primary school who told the infants class that Santa doesn't exist. Wullie was particularly upset by this latest revelation, as he'd already sent a letter off asking for his very own Danny Alexander glove puppet after George Osborne blagged the one the Lib Dems already had.

Our second invitation to ooh-aah-ery came courtesy of Wullie again, joined this time by Anas Sarwar, who's forever looking for a deflection strategy in case folk realise that the hereditary principle isn't the best way to select a Labour candidate. Although the offspring of Tony Blair, Neil Kinnock, John Prescott and Jack Straw may beg to differ. Anas is still hoping that he'll get Magrit Curran's job as Shadow Scottish Secretary after he stood down as deputy Scottish branch manager in order to remove one of the objections to the Smugurphy's candidacy - that Jim getting the gig would mean both leader and deputy were Westminster MPs, which would prove Johann's criticism that the party in Scotland was being dictated to by London - something we'd already guessed anyway.

Mind you there are a myriad of other objections to Smugurphy getting the job, not the least of which is that Jim Murphy is objectionable in and of himself. But Magrit would have to be replaced anyway. She is widely regarded as being ineffective as Shadow Scottish Secretary because no one in the Labour party is sure whether she's being sneery enough about the SNP. Her face looks like that all the time and no one can tell the difference.

Wullie and Anas were annoyed that three SNP cooncillors from East Renfrewshire had the temerity to mock the Smith Commission report by saying it was a worthless confection of lies and visually demonstrating this by setting fire to it and dumping it in a bin. It was behaviour every bit as mature as Wullie Rennie's, and at least had the advantage of providing something that you could toast some chestnuts on. Wullie's party has only got old chestnuts, in the form of ancient jokes like Jim Wallace and Ming Campbell.

Wullie immediately decided that the stunt was another test for Nicola, who disappointingly obliged him by condemning the SNP cooncillors. What she should have done of course would have been merely to point out that she had no time for childish behaviour and tantrums, whether they come from SNP cooncillors or the leader of the dwindling band of Lib Dems at Holyrood.

You really shouldn't pay Wullie Rennie any heed Nicola, unless it's to mock him, it only makes him think he's important and has something worthwhile to say. The last time Wullie made a substantive contribution to a debate was when he was mistaken for a bus driver and said, "No, you want the number 17 to Kelty."

There are going to be many more "Nicola Sturgeon accused" stories over the coming months. Perhaps one day this country will have a media which spends the same amount of time and energy fearlessly accusing Gordie Broon, but you won't be seeing that in the pages of the Daily Record or on the BBC - which is why we need sites like Wings Over Scotland. Wullie Rennie finding them objectionable is precisely why we need them.

Alicsammin's Part in Alan Cochrane's Downfall

7 December 2014

How many Alan Cochranes does it take to screw in a lightbulb? He doesn't have to, he just holds up the bulb and the world revolves around him. Alan has a very high conceit of himself, and indeed the man is remarkable as the field of journalism is indeed crowded with exceedingly large egos balanced precariously upon very little talent. Competing against contenders like Piers Morgan and Kelvin Mackenzie, the Telegraph's Scottish editor easily wins the prize for inflating oneself greater than a whoopee cushion designed for an elephantine backside, a feat previously managed only by Gordie Broon. Never in the history of newspaper opinionists has such a small mind occupied such a big head.

Alan's just published his memoirs, coming to a remainder bin near you very soon. To save you the bother of reading them, they essentially boil down to the claim that anyone who's anyone in Scottish Unionist politics, or UK politics, or the Pope, never does anything without first consulting Alan and benefitting from his words of wisdom. For yeah verily, seekers of union look unto the cockring, the sayer of sooths and the fount of all that is good and true, or at least Ruth Davidson. And this is why the Unionist parties are doing so terribly well these days in the affections of the Scottish electorate. No really. Alan said so.

Having won the referendum, mostly by making desperate last minute promises of vague and unspecified devomaxiness, the holiest prediction of the gaping cockring has perplexingly failed to come to pass. Alicsammin remains resolutely undownfallen. However much the cockring throws himself likes hoops in a fairground side show, the bobbing ducks of alicsamminry just keep dodging the devastation that is wrought in the pages of a Tory newspaper that no one reads outside of the Morningside Endangered Species Reservation for David Mundells and Action Krankie Abseilers. Alan can't understand why this should be, when all the really important people hang onto his every word like unpleasant berries on a bottom. Yet the plebby people with clean shiny bums continue to ignore him.

Far from downfalling, the Alicsammin promises to continue to be a trapped bawhair in the cockring for quite some time to come. It's a passion killer for any warring couples thinking of conjugating in a loveless union, a guarantee of eventual divorce which is even more effective than waking up of a morning and having to look at Alan's mug. In what was the perhaps the worst kept secret in Scottish politics since it was revealed that the Labour party isn't socialist after all, Alicsammin has announced that he's going to stand for the Westminster Parlie at the next General Election.

So we've now been told officially that the lubricant for the cockring's outpourings is going to thrust himself into the seat of Gordon. Which is a sentence you wouldn't otherwise get to read outside a gay porn mag. Sadly Alicsammin is not going to stand for election as the new MP for Kirkcaldy which is an immense pity because it would be so funny and dripping with ironic karma that no would be satirist would have to think of anything smart arsed to say for several months. All you'd have to do would be to say "Kirkcaldy", and guffaw. Alicsammin is instead going to stand for the constituency of Gordon in Aberdeenshire, whose current MP, Malcolm Bruce, is a Lib Dem who's retiring citing extreme old age and decreptitude. And he's still only a third as old as Ming Campbell and with considerably less dry rot.

Malcolm Bruce's would be Lib Dem successor, Christine Jardine, is fair beelin that the Alicsammin is blythely wandering in to shove her political career even further into oblivion than Danny Alexander's. Ms Jardine does not appear to be an avid devotee of Twitter, but on her Twitter feed the vast majority of her tweets or retweets have been attacks on the SNP, or Alicsammin, or Wings Over Scotland and/or its readers rather than any positive comments on what she or her party might have done. Although to be fair that runs the risk of reminding people that Danny Alexander exists.

Instead Ms Jardine has gone full out for the Labour strategy of being unable to open their gob without criticising the SNP about something. She is perhaps hoping that voters might mistake her for Magrit Curran, although it truly is a sign of the deep and indeed hopeless desperation of the Lib Dems that Magrit has become something to aspire to.

Not that things look any better for Labour. Magrit Curran's latest master stroke is to give a speech to a bunch of Labour hacks during which she will attack the SNP for not being progressive enough. Because Labour have used this tactic before and it's been working out so well for them. In case you were wondering, "progressive" apparently means : supporting the Iraq war, bailing out banks with public money, creating a culture of poorly paid casual jobs in which low pay and big employers are subsidised while the poor are penalised, privatisation, PPP, ATOS contracts, sooking up to defence contractors and schmoozing with nuclear weapons, and being in favour of even fewer powers being devolved to Holyrood than even the Conservatives are willing to countenance. So that's progressive in the sense of progressing ever closer to the definition of "Tory".

The opinion polls continue to look dire for all the Unionist parties. With every new Scottish poll, the outlook is bleaker. It's highly probable that Alicsammin will be the new MP for Gordon, and it's highly probable that the SNP will take a majority of Scottish seats. They may very well end up with more seats than the despised Lib Dems, who are about to receive a kicking south of the Border commensurate only with the kicking they are about to receive north of it. And that could see whoever wants to form the next government of the UK - we're looking at you, Eds Miliband and Balls - being dependent upon the goodwill and grace of Alicsammin. There's that ironic karma again.

It's highly probable that Alan Cochrane will live to see the Tory party, the Labour party, and the Lib Dems reduced to electoral insignificance and Alicsammin will achieve his goal of Scottish independence - not because it is the expressed and settled will of the Scottish people, but because all those Unionist party elites whom Alan fondly believes hang on to his every word are short-termist idiots following moronic advice from whoopee cushions with beards. Still, at least he can commiserate with Alistair Darling over a lovely home-made lasagne.

Running Down Shettleston Road Naked with a Red Rose Up My Bum

13 December 2014

I've come over all Labour party this week, scabby, lazy, and only interested in my own comfort. I've got an excuse - my psoriasis has flared up again - but the Labour party's condition is terminal. I decided we need to make labourparty a word - it describes self-absorbed selfish people who only do what suits themselves but who hypocritically make out that what suits them just so happens to be in the interests of everyone else and we ought to be grateful to them. But then I remembered there's already a word for that - and that word is jimmurphy.

I've been asked to do some public speaking and campaigning during the run up to the General Election. A friend who's involved with the SNP branch in Glasgow East has asked me to give a few speeches in support of their candidate - who has yet to be selected. Glasgow East is where I live and while I'm not an SNP member, it's only the SNP which has any chance of taking the seat from the inbumbent - no that's not a typo - the fragrant Magrit Curran (she reeks of complacency and entitlement). An imbumbent is a careerist seat-warmer, in case you were wondering. I'm not that keen on public speaking, but I agreed, because if it would help to separate Magrit from her expenses claims I'd run down Shettleston Road naked with a red rose up my bum while towing a life sized cardboard effigy of Jim Murphy and asking everyone I pass the only question of any relevance about the Smugurph - battery or free range?

My friend said she thought it might be wiser if I did a wee speech instead though.

Another Labour imbumbent is Frank Doran, MP for Aiberdeen North, or at least for the men. Frank is a byword for pomposity and entitlement, having pissed off the staff of the House of Commons some years ago when a committee he chaired ruled that MPs have the right to jump the queue in the canteen. Scottish Labour MPs are busy and important people, those expenses forms take ages to fill in you know.

Frank's in a spot of bother after he said in the Commons that the post of Fisheries Minister was not a job for a woman. He was clearly confused by the meaning of the feminist slogan: a woman without a man is like a fish without a bicycle. Mind you, a Scottish Westminster constituency without a Labour MP is like an intestine without a tapeworm. Anyway, in a botched attempt to get his foot out of his gob, Frank claimed that his remark wasn't sexist because he "knows the fishing industry" - so in other words it's the people who work in the fishing industry who are the sexist Neanderthals, not him. Frank's not sexist, he just thinks his constituents are. Well saved there then Frankie boy. Perhaps he could discuss it with the Norwegian Minister for Fisheries, Elisabeth Aspaker.

Of course the duties of the Fisheries Minister are not solely concerned with representing men on boats, the minister represents the entire fishing industry. There are many jobs within the industry which were traditionally filled by women - like filleting and gutting fish, shellfish, and molluscs like the Labour MP for Aiberdeen North.

But of course the big imbumbent news is the election of the Smugurph and Keezha the Daily Mail's Overcoat Pin Up as branch manager and deputy branch manager. Jim got 55.77% according to a press release which conveniently neglects to tell us what he got 55.77% of. In Labour's Byzantine system of voting where some people get three votes, this is by no means clear. 55.77% of apologists for Tony Blair? 55.77% of people whose brains have been surgically removed and replaced with a banana mush?

To make things a bit simpler, so that the likes of Magrit Curran or Frank Doran can understand them, it was also reported somewhere or other - I did have a link but the dug ate it - that 60.4% of Labour members voted for the Smugurph. This is not much better. 60.4% of what number? When you don't give a detailed breakdown of total votes cast, you are not reporting on a democratic election, you're reporting the result of a farce. 60.4% is meaningless unless we're told what it's 60.4% of. But then the Labour party in Scotland has been a meaningless farce for a very long time now, so I suppose it's appropriate.

So just how many people did actually vote for Jim Murphy? Labour doesn't want to tell us. No detailed breakdown of the votes has been published for the very good reason that it would reveal that the party Jim is leading most probably has fewer members than the number of employees of Scotmid. Scotmid employs over 5000 people in Scotland - how many active members does Labour have? This means that Scotmid branch managers are leaders in a bigger and far more influential organisation.

It is clear to everyone that a party only goes to such lengths to hide its membership figures if its membership figures are an embarrassment. Why else be so coy? If Labour had enjoyed a massive boost in membership following the referendum campaign that we are told Jim acquitted himself and free range hens so well in, the party would have been sure to tell us. It's equally an embarrassment that the supine Scottish media does not pursue them on this peculiar omission of information which is vital to the proper functioning of any supposedly democratic election. But fearlessly investigating how long it takes to turn a Labour press release into published copy by changing the intro and adding a couple of words at the end then accusing the SNP of something - that's the extent of the investigation that the Scottish media subjects Labour to. And they think we're impressed by this.

Labour's great hope for saving itself from the kicking they're about to receive for allowing the party to be taken over by right wing Westminster based careerists who are bereft of anything that can be described as a political principle is to choose as party branch manager a right wing Westminster based careerist who is bereft of anything that can be described as a political principle. A careerist who has received the support of an embarrassingly small number of people, the few who have yet to resign in disgust from a party which long ago lost anything that might pass for self-respect and replaced it with Magrit Curran.

But the Smugurph is the darling of the BBC and will be the subject of glowing reports from gushing reporters, and that's all that matters.

Thinking Very Carefully

18 December 2014

I'm plastered in potions and lotions in an attempt to get my psoriasis under control, but I'm not sure which is scabbier, psoriasis or the union. Psoriasis is a chronic condition, but there's a cure for the union even though we have yet to persuade a majority of Scottish voters that the side effects of the cure are nowhere near as bad as the disease. The cure may be some way off, and we don't yet have a date for our independence doctor's appointment, but at least the cure exists.

Another psoriatic Union lesion burst out onto the surface this week giving independence supporters something to scratch, with the revelations that the Queen's supposedly spontaneous non-intervention in the referendum debate was neither spontaneous nor a non-intervention. Well, I say revelation, this is one of those revelations like the revelation that the X-Factor is nothing more than a money making machine for Simon Cowell and not actually a means of nurturing genuine talent. It's a shocking surprise that anyone with half a brain knew at the time was a set up job, but saying so would only have brought down a torrent of accusations of tinfoil hattery from the Unionists who dominate the media. The usual suspects would have chorused "ooooh get her" in unison like a drag queen boy band dressed as girl band who'd just been turned down by Simon Cowell on the grounds that they were more butch than Louis Walsh.

Anyway, so Liz's office got a phone call from Davie Cameron's office, begging her to do something, anything, to help prevent Scottish people from voting for independence. We're dealing here with the rarefied world of people who employ people to answer their personal telephones, because protocol dictates that you can't just give Liz a call on her mobile and tell her that her operating system is infected with the virus of nationalism. Davie's spad doubtless reminded the royal flunky on the other end of the phone that Scottish people are well known connoisseurs of vodka which they will cheerfully consume without crackers. Actually he probably didn't, because he probably thinks we only drink whisky and isn't very clear on the distinction between Irn Bru and Tizer.

Some have attempted to defend Liz's intervention on the grounds that remarking that people should "think very carefully" before they vote is not in itself an attempt to influence the outcome. I'd ask such people to think very carefully before they open their gobs. You do not ask people to "think very carefully" before making a decision if you genuinely do not give a toss what decision people will reach. Imploring that a person should "think very carefully" is the sort of response that you give to an elderly and wealthy relative with no weans who's just told you she's considering leaving all her money to the Maryhill Food Bank and the Cute Yes Supporting Spanish Mongrel Foundation and isn't going to leave it all to you so you can buy that large Highland estate you've always wanted and teach baby Prince George how to shoot Bambi's mammy.

Clearly, Queeniepoos cares deeply, and equally clearly, would prefer we voted No. Because anyone with half a brain, even people with a quarter of a brain, in fact even Alan Cochrane, understands very well that an independent Scottish Parliament is far more likely to vote for a referendum on the future of the monarchy than the Westminster Parliament is. And Liz knows that too. She knows that as soon as she pops her clogs, an independent Scottish Parliament would be faced with a clamour for a referendum from hundreds of thousands of Scottish people who would rather have a potato as head of state than King Charles III. Although it wouldn't really be that easy to tell the difference. On balance the potato would be better, because it could at least be distilled into vodka. The only thing you'd distil from Charles is an overpriced organic cracker and a flunky whose job is to squeeze toothpaste on the brush.

So having prevailed upon the Royals of the desperate need for an intervention that wasn't an intervention really, Liz obliged with a wee charade involving getting the polis to position the waiting media in the exact place so they'd just happen to overhear Liz making a carefully rehearsed and choreographed spontaneous remark which was written and prepare by some Tory government official. A remark which didn't contain any bias in its text, only in its subtext, providing a fig leaf of plausible denial. And moreover one which was conveniently disguised as an overheard private conversation, giving Liz the excuse not to comment on any uncomfortable or difficult questions that might arise in the future. Questions like - so you did stick yer highly privileged oar in even though you know that's a no-no, didn't you? Or questions like - you do know that the Scottish people reserve the right to get rid of monarchs that piss them off, don't you? Or questions like - oh come on, you're not saying you really take Alan Cochrane seriously, are you?

You can argue about how neutral the Queen's comments were from now until the Sun has fused the last of its hydrogen into helium atoms and expanded into a red giant and consumed the Earth, or until Scotland has forgiven the Labour party for giving the Royal family a run for its money in the sense of entitlement states - my money is on the Sun - but you can't deny that the entire episode was manipulative, underhand, conniving, immoral, and dishonest. Even though it achieved in its immediate purpose - to assist the chances of a No vote - it still managed to be woefully inept because it got found out and so has only damaged its longer term interests due to its own short-sighted manoeuvring. All of which is, come to think of it, a pretty good description of the workings of the Westminster Parliament, and the longer term fate of the Union, so there's a poetic circularity to it all.

In much the same way, this week Davie Cameron's wheeze to use the result of the Scottish referendum as a political tool to head UKIP off at the pass and get one up over Labour fell apart around his ears. Operating for short term advantage leads to longer term failure - and in the case of the constitutional status of Scotland in the Union, the time bought by the short term manoeuvring gets shorter and shorter. Back in the 1950s, the short term manoeuvring that dismissed the two million strong petition of the Scottish Covenant bought Westminster nearly 30 years of kicking Scotland into the long grass, the 40% rule in the referendum of 1979 bought 18 years, and the referendum of 1997 bought Westminster 17 years. Yet despite the fact that Westminster won the referendum of 2014, they couldn't even manage a couple of months. The Scottish lion is very much out of the long grass, and eyeing a devomax haunch and licking its lips. Westminster's ungulates are looking on nervously.

In other news - I need a job. I've been subtle. I've dropped hints. I've coquettishly fluttered my eyelids, and trust me, coquettish is not a look that looks good on me, but I'm still awaiting the offer of a regular column in certain newly founded national newspapers. Newly founded national newspapers that could be doing with a wee more in the way of funny and not taking yourself that seriously. More in the way of miniature erythrismal canids, in fact. Because it's not just Kevin McKenna that can write fancy words, oh no.

National newspapers aside. I really do need a job. I don't propose boring you with my financial issues, but I didn't inherit any pensions after my other half passed away, and I gave up work in order to care for him. So unless I can find a lasting means of supporting myself, there won't be any blog articles because I'll be too busy asking "Big Issue?" to passers by in the street. Well maybe not, because I do at least have my own house. But I need to eat. And to pay the bills.

I'm 52, have an impressive line in vintage suits, and speak fluent Spanish. I formerly worked as the editor of a monthly English language magazine in Spain. Very much the low rent end of the publishing trade, but it taught me how to write to a deadline. Prior to that I worked in the voluntary sector. Ideally I'd like a part time job, anything I can do sitting on my bum in an office - or even working from home. Except a call centre, or sales. And I'm too old for the outdoorsy stuff, or heavy lifting.

Mr Hi-Jumpy and the High Jump

23 December 2014

Jim Murphy has been raising the profile of the Labour party this week, at least according to an interview in the Guardian, a newspaper which sells only a handful of copies in Scotland, most of which are to people who like the crossword. This means that the Labour party's profile has been successfully raised amongst people who like to do crosswords - but of course people who like to do crosswords also understand that 'deluded Mr Hi Jumpy is very confused (3, 6)'.

Anyway, Mr Hi Jumpy has a very high opinion of himself and likes to remind everyone how hard it was for him when he was a baba. The Baby Hi Jumpy was born in a cutlery drawer in Arden under a star, or at least a disco ball, and was visited by the three kings from Labour party headquarters who presented him with the gifts of a brass neck, a press office, and an expenses claims form. Mainly in the hope it would make him go away and stop plotting against Ed Miliband.

However the media is determined to blur the distinction in the voter's mind between Jim Murphy and the Baby Jesus, and over the coming holiday season BBC Scotland has lined up a Christmas special programme called Jim's Nativity Miracle, during which he'll be visited by a donkey, an ass, and some shepherds who've lost their sheep - that'll be Ian Davidson and Dougie Alexander together with the management of BBC Scotland. Kezia Dugdale will play the role of an angel in a dufflecoat, who appears in a vision to the Daily Mail and complains about cybernats being nasty to her.

The Christmas message will be that Mr Hi Jumpy has come to redeem Labour from its sins, and seeks to achieve this by hoping that the rest of us will forget what Labour's many sins are if we're constantly bombarded with sycophantic interviews which go on about drawers in Arden like it makes Jim something special. It might spoil the infantile narrative to point out that Jim's hardships largely took place during a time when Labour was in power, and the policies Jim and the rest of his misbegotten party have espoused ever since have done precious little to alleviate them for the rest of the residents of Arden. Labour, let us recall, refused to allow the devolution of minimum wage policy to the Scottish Parliament during the Smith commission negotiations.

Mr Hi Jumpy told the Guardian's reporter that it was clear from the attacks on him that his opponents think he "isn't shit". And this would be true, Jim's opponents don't think he's shit. But just stick an indefinite article in front of that last noun and you've got a very accurate assessment of what we do think he is. The chain is going to be pulled in May, and the 45 campaign is lining up to perform the role of the toilet duck of Scottish politics.

In his latest foray into lookitme politics, Mr Hi Jumpy has announced that he wants to end the ban on alcohol at fitba matches. He thinks it's unfair that middle class yobs at rugby matches can imbibe some swally, but working class yobs at the real fitba can't. Jim's teetotal himself, but he's drunk on the idea of cheap publicity, and he needs all the cheap publicity he can get, because according to the opinion polls Labour continues to look like a down and out alkie in the electoral gutter. The UK media kept telling us that Jim was going to turn around the fortunes of the Labour party, how a big hitter like him was exactly what the party needed to take on the supposedly provincial politicians of Holyrood, but it's not working out according to plan, despite the hagiographies and near sainthood bestowed on a serial expenses claimant and apologist for Tony Blair's war crimes.

But Jim is no longer an apologist - he thinks Labour needs to stop apologising and move on. Politicians always say this sort of thing when they desperately hope that the public will overlook their previous lies and misleading statements and will listen enthusiastically to the next lot of lies and misleading statements. Jim might be done apologising, but that certainly doesn't mean that the public has forgiven him and the rest of his unapologetic elves and dwarves.

A sign that considerably more apologising and crawling will have to be done by Labour came in the latest Scottish opinion poll, fieldwork for which came after Jim was crowed about and crowned. The headline figures can be summarised as : Labour's going to get a kicking that will make the massed ranks of the Can Can dancers at the Moulin Rouge look like they're wearing shackles. Labour is going to get kicked from Caithness all the way to Jim's holy Celtic park and from there to Galloway, then back again. Done apologising? If they had any sense they'd know they've not even started - but then when did Labour in Scotland ever have any sense? A sense of entitlement, certainly, common sense, not a bit of it.

In a statement that's going to come back to haunt him, Mr Hi Jumpy keeps repeating his assertion that Labour won't lose a single seat to the SNP in the Westminster General Election due in May. He's almost certainly going to be proven right, Labour won't lose a single seat to the SNP, it looks set to lose dozens.

But undaunted, Mr Hi Jumpy claims, "[Labour's opponents] have got to work out how they deal with the argument we're going to make, which is you can protest against Cameron by voting for the Greens or the Nats, but you can only replace him with one party."

Well that's easy isn't it - we'll deal with the argument by pointing out that how Scotland votes can't replace the Tories anyway, as 50 useless Labour MPs have proven repeatedly. If voters in England want a Tory government, they'll get a Tory government. But in Scotland we can vote SNP or Green and get MPs who won't support Tory austerity policies and who will not go into coalition with or support the Tories at Westminster. MPs who will vote for what is in the best interests of Scotland. 50 Magrit Currans and Jim Murphies voting for austerity policies and what's good for the banks - or 50 MPs working for Scotland and Scotland's interests? Hardly a difficult choice, is it.

Mr Hi Jumpy's for the high jump.

Giving Up Bad Habits

26 December 2014

've given up smoking, it's not always easy giving up ciggies even though you don't get much pleasure from it. Over a month now without polluting my lungs with the evil weed, and I've also joined the ranks of thousands of Scots who've kicked the bad habit - that would be the bad habit of voting Labour. I used to vote Labour, but then I realised it causes cancer of the Scottish body politic and leads to the premature death of aspirations.

By an eerie coincidence, the percentage of Scottish voters who say they plan to vote Labour at the next election is more or less the same as the percentage of Scottish adults who still smoke. But giving up one is a whole lot easier than giving up the other. The main difference being that while former smokers still get cravings for a fag, no one in their right mind feels a desire to have a sook on Jim Murphy. Not even Anas Sarwar.

Labour's been a bad habit in Scottish politics for far too long. We voted Labour without thinking as we wrongly believed it was the only way to keep the Tories out of office. But the truth of the matter is that the only way to keep the Tories out of office is for voters in England not to vote for them, and there's precious little that the

Scottish electorate can do to influence that. For all Labour's calls for solidarity with folk south of the border during the referendum campaign, there's precious little solidarity in the other direction. Voters vote according to what they consider to be in their own best interests, and if voters in England believe their interests are best served by voting Tory, no appeals to solidarity with Caledonians are going to make them do otherwise.

We voted Labour all the way through the 80s and 90s, and got Tory governments anyway. We voted Labour in 1997 and got a Labour government that had become Red Tory in order to appeal to voters in England because that was the only way it could get elected. So Scottish voters must take a leaf out of our English brothers and sisters' book, and vote according to what is in our own best interests. Vote for parties that put Scotland first. That doesn't mean we let the Tories in, no party which puts Scotland first is going to ally itself with David Cameron and George Osborne. But Labour will adopt Cameron and Osborne's policies in an effort to appeal to voters in the English shires. Eds Miliband and Balls have already said they'll implement the same austerity plan, just with a sad face and a more adenoidal commentary.

Scotland needs to break the Labour habit, and during the referendum campaign hundreds of thousands of us gave it up as we saw Labour stand shoulder to shoulder with the Tories and wrap itself in the Union flag and cheer as bosses, bankers and big business issued dire warnings and threats at the behest of Westminster. Scotland is too small to go it alone, our economy too unbalanced and weak, they told us, conveniently sidestepping the question that if what they said was true, then it made little sense to continue to vote for the pathetic parties which had brought about this lamentable state of affairs. We've made you rubbish, Labour cried, so vote for us. Labour is no longer the people's party, they're the party of managing the people's expectations on behalf of the banks and the bosses.

Labour may once have had principles, but now the party is epitomised by the man most likely to take over as branch manager in Scotland, Jim Murphy. It's not true to say that the Smugurphy has no guiding political principles, he does, and they are clear and consistent and can be summarised in three words - and those words are "Jim Murphy's career".

Since the referendum, Labour's support has gone into freefall while support for pro-Scotland parties like the SNP, the Greens and the SSP has shot upwards. Due to the distorting features of the first past the post voting system, it now looks quite possible that Labour will be reduced to a tiny rump of Scottish seats, a backside that's been severely kicked. We need to make sure this comes to pass, if Scottish voters can ensure that the Unionist parties lack a majority of Scottish seats then we can effectively block any claim to democratic legitimacy of any attempt by Westminster to tinker with the devolution settlement. And if the SNP were the third or fourth largest party in Westminster then pro-Scotland parties could be key to the stability of a future UK government. That's the way to extract concessions, not by voting Labour and hoping that they'll pay us heed when they've never paid us any heed in the past.

Once you've broken a bad habit, and realised it was nothing more than a bad habit, you start to see the benefits. In the case of giving up smoking you find your lung capacity increases - which is extremely useful for screaming abuse at the telly at a greater volume whenever Magrit Curran's mug hoves into view - and your bank balance is a whole lot healthier too. In the few short weeks since stopping smoking, I reckon I've saved over £300. And in the few short weeks since Scotland's broken the Labour habit, it looks like we can save an entire country.

Skanktimonious Sock Puppets and the Smugurph Bounce

4 January 2015

It's not easy being Saint Dougie the Diminutive, all those party colleagues and Guardian writers looking at you expecting a miracle, and all you've got is a box of party tricks that are as transparent as cling film on a mouldy piece and cheese. The poor wee lambie can't even stand on a box to make himself look more imposing, not since the Smugurph blagged it to go off on his eggy magnetic tour and the Kirk of Scotland hasn't obliged him with a pulpit for ages. Labour's very own wee skanktimonious sock puppet has been bouncing up and down excitedly in the columns of the Guardian again - because Severin Carroll is on his holidays and the paper has to mainline Labour press releases instead of cutting it with filler to pretend that they're publishing their own copy.

The occasion of Dougie's holier than thou bouncing was the news that during the next General Election the Tories - boo hiss - are set to outspend Labour - boo hiss - by a factor of three to one. This is because the Tories are even more successful at whoring themselves out to big business than Labour is, news which comes as something as a surprise to anyone who has followed Jim Murphy's career or who has realised why skanktimonious isn't a typo when it's applied to Dougie Alexander. But undaunted, St Dougie the Dwaarfie, patron saint of crotchless knickers, is promising that Labour is going to beat the Tories in the ground war and will outnumber Tory activists by the same margin on the streets and chapping on the doors.

To be fair, this will not be hard to achieve in Dougie's constituency where the Tories can be outnumbered three to one by Dougie, his alter ego as a creeping Jesus, and his sister. That is if his sister is still talking to him, but the knife that he plunged into Wendy's back does act as a very convenient hanger for election posters. In Dougie's constituency and across the rest of Scotland, outnumbering the Tories isn't difficult. Pandas have famously achieved it. The difficulty will be outnumbering the SNP, who have been breeding prodigiously and are to Labour as rabbits are to pandas. The Tory activists are demoralised, says Dougie, who has clearly confused them with his own dwindling band of unhappy Labour campers.

Not that anyone really knows how many activists Labour has in Scotland, since the party refused to release the full voting figures from their coronation of St Jim the Haloed. What we do know is that there are 475 elected Labour representatives in Scotland - MPs, MSPs, MEPs, and local councillors, so if active party membership is indeed around the 7000 mark as estimated by Stu Campbell on Wings Over Scotland, then 6.8% of Labour's active members are elected politicians, and a sizeable whack of the remainder are either related to them or are their personal friends. Allowing for each elected representative to have a significant other and at least six relatives or friends - although in the case of Ian Davidson that's probably stretching it considerably - then 54.4% of the Labour party in Scotland is made up of elected Labour politicians and their personal contacts. No wonder they were too embarrassed to release the actual figures. Labour in Scotland isn't a party, it's a private members club. That explains the crotchless knickers then.

Anyway, Dougie is determined that Labour is going to surf the tidal wave of public anger and that's going to carry them to victory, neglecting to take into account the fact that much of that public anger is directed at Dougie and his pals. So Labour will indeed be surfing the wave, in much the same way that the Titanic surfed that iceberg, straight down to the bottom of a mid-Atlantic trench with no way out.

Dougie tells us that Labour is "engaging with the anger", although he's not actually explained how. As a voter in Magrit Curran's constituency, I have yet to witness anything that might lead me to believe that Magrit was engaging with the anger of local people - something she could achieve quite easily by being locked into a pillory at Parkhead Cross and having stale yum yums, custard pies, and past their sell by date cream cakes thrown at her. But nothing with jam in it, because Labour would combust spontaneously if it was ever confronted with real jam. Jam and Labour have never been seen together in the same room. Jam is Labour's kryptonite. Only invisible mythical jam does it for Labour. And definitely not eggs. Eggs are vile and dangerous weapons of hatred and souflé destruction. You could have someone's eye out with a flan. Just ask Jim Murphy. His entire career is built on egg based aggression.

Meanwhile the Smugurph himself has been touting his inventive auld schtick again. No, not his expenses claims, the claim that we need to vote Labour in order to keep out Davie Cameron. In Coatbridge and Methil - are there any Tories in Coatbridge and Methil? Voting Labour to keep out the Tories worked so well the last time, didn't it, and Jim wants us to stick with a winning strategy. Winning for him, that is, the rest of us are screwed anyway. I seem to recall that we voted en masse for Labour at the General Election in 2010, Scotland returned 50 odd Labour MPs to Westminster - and in some cases they were extremely odd indeed, Wullie Bain, 'nuff said - and we signally failed to keep out Davie Cameron. However we did give Magrit Curran and the Smugurph some lovely expenses claims and a John Lewis list, so it was all worthwhile really.

Scotland voted Labour all the way through the 1980s and 90s, and we didn't keep the Tories out. We voted Labour in 2010, and we didn't keep the Tories out. Vote Labour to keep out the Tories is one of the most pernicious myths of Scottish politics. Apart from the myth that Labour is a left wing party and Jim Murphy is a socialist. Voting for an anti-Tory party like the SNP or the Greens is not going to increase Davie Cameron's chances of electoral success, it's not going to make a Tory government more likely. An SNP, or Scottish Green or Scottish Socialist MP (OK, so I can dream) is not going to support a Cameron government. And neither, unlike Jim

Murphy's Labour party, would they support Labour's Tory austerity with a sad face policies.

Despite the frantic spinning of the likes of Dougie and the Scottish media, Labour has not enjoyed a bounce in the polls following the election of Jim Murphy as branch manager. We've seen Labour's promises far too often before, and this time we see through the spin and the cant. 2015 looks like it's going to be a momentous year. It's going to be the year that Labour finally gets the message that Scottish voters have been sending it for the best part of ten years now. They'll get the message when we vote the sorry lot of them out of office and replace them with politicians who prioritise the interests of Scotland and Scottish communities, not the City of London, the banks, and the defence industry. And no amount of excited spinning from a skanktimonious intellectual dwarf will change that. The Smugurph bounce is Labour's final leap into a well-deserved oblivion.

Happy New Year Dougie.

Mortuary SLAB

11 January 2015

I've given up - my plans to write about something other than the flustercluck which passes for the Smugurph's leadership of the Labour party in Scotland have foundered upon the McTernan Rocks, a diminutive and unpleasant excrescence in the barren sea of Blair which previously sank the career of the leader of the Labour party in Australia, and dragged into the murky depths by the slimy tentacles of the cataclysmic Robertson monster with its remarkably small mouth.

Much as I criticise the Labour party in Scotland, I had assumed that they had an organ approximating a brain which permitted them to engage in a modicum of strategic planning. A wrong-headed brain, a selfish brain, a self-serving and hypocritical brain perhaps, but it was reasonable to assume that somewhere deep within the bowels of Labour party lurked something which could be described as grey matter. But no, there's just more crap and a fetid odour. You'll find plastic toys of infinitely greater value in a Christmas cracker, as well as jokes that are less stale. Labour only gives us plastic toys like Wee Wullie Bain, and bad jokes like Magrit Curran.

The deeply gobsmacky thing is that Labour is after all a party which aspires to govern the Yookayohkay, and so you could be forgiven for believing that they must have some notion of the complexities of the task before them. But you'd be sadly wrong. The Labour party in Scotland is brain dead. The only grey matter they have is corpse grey on the mortuary SLAB. All they are interested in is trying, by whatever means necessary, to persuade enough information deprived suckers to mark an X by their candidate in the next election. They don't have a clue what they propose to do with power once they achieve it - other than, of course, to keep getting those salaries and expense accounts, and angling for cushy directorships once their political careers are spent. What Labour won't be doing is anything that approaches the redistribution of wealth and power.

It's hard to imagine what reason a sentient body interested in responsible socialist tinged government might have had for appointing John McTernan, dwarfy pitbull stand-in and purveyor of jaggy underwear for Tony Blair, as the chief of staff for the Labour party in Scotland. John is the embodiment of just about everything that has revolted people and turned them off Labour over the past couple of decades. John represents a Labour party which is unremittingly negative, sneering, dismissive, and possessed of an overweening sense of its own righteousness which it believes provides more than ample justification for its childish vindictiveness.

John's great political theory was the notion that the only way to beat the Tories at the ballot box is to out-Tory them. So he enthusiastically spun and smeared for a party that tacked ever further to the right. People like John believe that hating the Tories means it's OK to be hateful, and in his hatred fails to realise that he has turned into the very thing he hates. The irony is of course lost on him. John doesn't do irony. He doesn't do empathy, compassion, or understanding either. That's what makes him the perfect right hand man for Jim Murphy.

John was most likely behind the utterly ridiculous claim that under the Smugurph, Labour would recruit 1000 more nurses in Scotland than the SNP, and these nurses would be funded by a raid on a tax on London properties. It's the kind of nastiness favoured by John, who naturally assumes that everyone else is as revolting as he is. The underlying assumption is of course that Labour supporters were attracted to vote Yes because they hate the English, and so can be persuaded to return to Labour if Labour promises to punish the English - especially those in London. The policy is of course an utter nonsense, but it grabbed the headlines, so job done.

Health is a devolved matter, so no number of Westminster MPs is going to make the slightest bit of difference. The only way that Jim's nursing pledge could come to pass is if Labour wins an outright victory in May 2015 in Westminster and May 2016 in Holyrood. Good luck with that Jim. Meanwhile Labour politicians from London accused Jim of trying to buy Scottish votes by damaging the party's chances of succeeding in gaining votes in London - where it also needs to succeed if there is any chance of it forming a government in 2015. Ed Miliband must be rueing the day that he decided to back the Smugurph for Scottish leadership and wondering if

Sarah Boyack or Neil Findlay would have been so bad after all.

The lovely John tweeted on Friday that his appointment had been condemned by the usual suspects - that would presumably be you and me then - but welcomed by the "right people". And this is perfectly true, right people were hugely enthused, John's appointment was widely welcomed by right wing commentators who write for the Telegraph.

John's strategy for Labour is founded on the need to bring "Glasgow man" back to the party. "Glasgow man" is shorthand for West of Scotland male voters, who traditionally backed Labour, but who voted Yes in the referendum. People like me then. But if John McTernan thinks I am going to be attracted by his vindictiveness and his negativity, he's in for a rude shock. I'm not interested in "sticking the boot into London" John. I'm interesting of ridding politics of nasty wee trolls like you.

It's even harder to imagine the thought processes engaged in by the person who wrote the press release saying that the Scottish Labour party would henceforth put the needs of Scotland first when developing policy. Apparently they were unaware that this was an admission that they've not put Scotland's need first up until now - although admittedly this comes under the heading "so tell us something we don't know". All this was bad enough - but what on earth possessed them to tell the papers that the party had christened the new doctrine Murphy's Law? Don't they know what that means?

There hasn't been a less appropriate name since General Motors launched a marketing campaign to sell a car called the Nova in Mexico, unaware that *No Va* is Spanish for "it doesn't go". Labour doesn't even have the excuse that they are operating in a foreign language. Unless you count honesty, but that's not a foreign language to them, just a foreign concept.

Whoops There Go My Neurones

17 January 2015

I went to visit a friend last night, who insisted that she had to watch her favourite telly show - Celebrity Big Brother. Katie Hopkins is in it, taking refuge from that part of the Scottish population which is overcome with the urge to force feed her a Mars bar deep fried in ebola. Which is to say about 5 million of us. But don't let it be said that you cannot learn something from a telly show which is to intellectual insight as a Labour party manifesto is to political philosophy. I learned that there really are people on this planet who are more vacuous and attention seeking than Katie Hopkins, and not all of them are elected representatives of the Labour party in Scotland like Mr High Jumpy. Although to be fair, he's still way more inflated than anything put into Katie Price by a plastic surgeon.

But after a wee while I could feel neurones in my brain giving up and taking early advantage of the Scottish Parliament's proposals for assisted suicide. I'd not felt my IQ drop so rapidly since having the immense misfortune to watch Prime Minister's Questions earlier in the week. This week's Parliamentary bonfire of the synapses consisted of Davie Cameron and Ed Miliband each telling the other that they were either a chicken or were feart.

Or rather 'frit' in Westminsterspeak, because they've always got everything Rs-first over elbow.

The topic of the yah-booh suckery being Davie telling Ed that he wasn't going to take part in any televised debates before the election unless Caroline Lucas of the English and Welsh Green party got a chance to trade insults too. Ed said that this made Davie a free-market chicken, and Davie retorted that Ed was a chicken fritter, and another little bit of British democracy died along with a few tens of thousands of synapses. Westminster Parliamentary debates are even less satisfying than that wee pang of disappointment which you get when you take a swig from your mug of tea only to discover that you'd already finished it.

This development has nothing to do with Davie's pre 2010 electoral commitment to be the greenest government ever, a commitment which went much the same way as the commitment of the Lib Dems not to raise student fees - and buggered off in the same ministerial motor. Davie's new-found fondness for fecund Greenery has a lot more to do with countering the disadvantage he feels at being out-reactionaried by the grinning mug of Nigel to his right. So Davie wants the Lib Dems and Labour to have to deal with a leftish party which does actually possess some principles. It's not so much that this will make Davie's lack of principles look any more like he might actually have some principles, as it will help to drag Nick and Ed down into the murky depths of unprincipled Torydom alongside the other bottom feeders.

The only surprising thing about any of this being that Davie was worried that other people might have a high opinion of Ed or Nick that needed to be brought down a bit in public estimation. But then none of them ever spend much time in the company of normal human beings and naturally their views about what normal people think are about as accurate as Magrit Curran's views on what constitutes a good telephone voice.

Naturally none of the parties involved really give a toss about the inclusivity of our political process. Neither do they much care about ensuring that the electorate is fully informed of the range of democratic choices before them. But mostly they were fully in agreement that that Nicola shouldn't be allowed anywhere near the proceedings. We'll be having none of that nasty Scottish separatism spoiling a perfectly yah boo debate with that being principled stuff. Besides, they've heard how during the independence referendum she shredded a couple of Scottish secretaries and met Johann Lamont full on in stairheid rammying, and would, if pressed and received cast iron assurances that it was deffo off the record, confess in private that they wet their pants a wee bit at the thought of the prospect. And not in a sexy way.

But Nicola isn't going to be allowed anyway, because despite the No vote in the indy referendum, being Scottish isn't quite British enough. You can be the biggest party in Scotland, you can be the only party in Scotland, but unless you stand for election somewhere that people who write for the politics pages of the Daily Mail can actually pronounce, then you're not properly British.

Middlesbrough or Melton Mowbray yes, Milngave or Mauchline no.

The debates and the pointless point-scoring it generates only highlights the problem of a media which still thinks it's the media of a centralised state. Yet Scotland is one of the constituent parts of Britain is it not - the BBC said so. An equal partner in the most successful union of nations in the history of anything narrated by Simon Schama.

But if there was a Scottish national broadcaster then the issue would be less politically toxic, because then we could have equal airtime given to the parties that people here are plausibly going to vote for. But the Scottish broadcast media is as toothless and senile as the Labour party which was its first and only true love and the Tories who constitute the official pantomime villains.

And this is why we are in the most peculiar state of affairs that no one finds it peculiar that the heid bummer of BBC Scotland hasn't made it known that the leaders of leading political parties in Scotland ought to have the same right to representation in a British political debate as do leaders of purplish parties voted for by people in Purley or Penge. A whole lot of pee there, but then we are talking about UKIP and BBC Scotland. BBC Scotland is in fact exactly like the Scottish Labour party it fawns over so desperately. Neither of them actually exist.

So it turns out that the topic that has most bothered our political masters this week is the question of whether an imaginary broadcaster should host imaginary debates for imaginary political parties so that newspapers that no one reads can spin the proceedings in imaginary ways. And then they wonder why people are turned off and want to build a new political system from scratch. Even the brain dead denizens of Celebrity Big Brother aren't that removed from the real world. Whoops, there go some more neurones.

A Diminishing Pile of Beans

23 January 2015

I t's been one of those weeks. I've not been very well, but am slowly getting better thanks to some nasty medicine. This is more than can be said for the ailing Labour party in Scotland, which on top of its deeply unattractive warts and acne, its sclerosis and its mange, is now showing all the symptoms of dysentery. That must be that Murphy bounce they keep telling us about then. Labour are just nasty, and no medicine can cure them.

A new opinion poll places the SNP on a whopping 52% for voting intention in the Westminster General election, a figure which would see the party walk off with all but four of Labour's seats in Scotland. The SNP would even take Mr Hi Jumpy's seat too, leaving the Scottish branch manager without an elected position and therefore, according to Labour's rulebook, he'd have to resign as Keezha's boss. But then Labour's rulebook exists mainly for the benefit of Labour's leadership, so doubtless a fudge would be found. Or if not a fudge then at least some tablet or a teacake, as Jim's so very very keen to establish his Scottish creds.

Jim was most recently seen on the telly today volunteering for a foodbank and hoping that no one would notice that it was policies he supported when in government that brought about the need for foodbanks to begin with. Jim Murphy helped to destroy the ability of thousands of folk to earn a living wage, but now he's helping to deliver a tin of beans on the telly. So that makes up for everything.

But the main news on Thursday was the sooper dooper tin of beans given to Scotland, on loan mind, by the Smith Commission. It's a lovely tin of beans, not as big a tin as the one we thought we were getting of course, but then Scottish people can't really be trusted with bean governing. We might not consume them after all, leading to copious amounts of Westminster gas, we might plant them and they could turn out to be magic beans which grow into a mighty bean plant leading to a magical land. Before you know it the sound of Fi Fie Foe Fum I smell the blood of Davie Cameron would be ringing out across the country. This is not a risk Westminster is prepared to take.

The Unionist parties have played a blinder in the Smith Commission, in the sense that they can't see where they're going and they don't know where they've been. It started with a vow to deliver the homiest ruliest devoest maxiest the world had ever seen. Scotland was going to get the most powerful devolved parliament in the history of devolved parliaments - although it still wouldn't have control of broadcasting, oil revenues, or most taxes and would have fewer powers than the Faroe Islands - population 49,000.

The bean pile was further reduced during negotiations, as Labour, Tory and Lib Dem bean counters on the phone to their London headquarters vied to remove a mung here and a haricot there. Labour didn't want Scotland to have control over abortion laws or the minimum wage. The Tories didn't want Scotland have control of anything much really, and the Lib Dems were just pleased that they got a ride in a ministerial motor.

Now the official bill has been put before Westminster, and a few more flageolets and favas have been removed from the pile. Scotland isn't going to get control of welfare powers after all. The Scottish Secretary is to get a veto. The Scottish Parliament can only take action on benefits policies after due "consultations" with the Scottish Secretary of State. This is a bit like a teenager being told that they can decide for themselves when they go to bed, but only after asking permission to stay up late from their mammy.

Anyway, if you've got a masochistic streak greater than that found in someone who gets his jollies from nailing his scrotum to a plank with rusty nails, you can read the entire document on the government's website. It consists of 134 pages of management-wankspeak which promise vague nothingness, and which will in any case be further diluted in interminable committee meetings in Westminster. By the time an Act passes its final reading, Scotland will be left with control of road signs and precious little else. Its sole purpose is to give the Conservatives an excuse to introduce measures to prevent Scottish MPs from voting on "English only" laws, even though, due to the Barnett Formula, those "English only" laws very often determine the overall level of Scottish funding.

This is why it is vitally important at the next General Election that Scotland's voters give the Unionist parties a kicking like they've never had before - and this essentially means we deprive Labour of their Scottish beans.

Labour counters this by claiming that Scotland needs to vote for them in order to keep out David Cameron, even though we voted Labour last time and got David Cameron anyway. It's pretty obvious that Scotland voting for Labour doesn't keep David Cameron out, we have David Cameron as Prime Minister to provide the evidence for that. Scotland voting SNP or Green increases the number of Tory seats in Westminster by precisely zero. David Cameron might think it's in his interests to destroy Labour in Scotland - but Labour's doing a perfectly grand job of destroying itself in Scotland all by itself.

But it's only by returning a majority of pro-Scotland MPs to Westminster in May that Scotland can ensure that our interests will be represented. Labour MPs put party interest first. It means that whatever machinations and manoeuvrings Westminster indulges in over Scottish devolution - and it's a given that they will - will not enjoy the support of a majority of Scotland's MPs and will lack a democratic mandate in Scotland. It means that Scottish MPs have a real chance of holding the balance of power and then we can ensure that the Unionists really do deliver on their promises to bring in Home Rule. And remember - home rule means at a very minimum that you get to control the TV remote control or it means nothing at all.

Vote Labour, vote to be powerless, vote for a diminishing pile of beans.

Magrit Fracks with the Truth

28 January 2015

Magrit Curran, my lovely MP, has a tangential relationship to truth, reality, and indeed her electorate. On Monday the fragrant one - she reeks of hypocrisy and stinks of the rot of a socialism that died a long time ago - tweeted that she had voted to stop fracking. She had of course done no such thing, Magrit had abstained on an SNP and Green backed motion to have a moritorium on fracking. She had voted for a Labour motion to allow fracking, subject to a few minor qualifications that will not unduly trouble the energy companies. It's a bit like claiming you've voted to ban television when you've supported a small increase in the licence fee, or saying that you've voted to ban smoking when you've abstained on a measure to introduce plain packaging.

But that's Magrit for you, she tells you she lives in the East End when she means she lives in a posh hoose in Newlands over the river. When questioned on the discrepancy between the facts and what actually come out of her gob, Magrit claims she represented the aspirations of East Enders - who apparently aspire to live somewhere else. Or possibly, like Magrit, we aspire not to remember where we live. Life in the East End after decades of Labour misrule is so depressing that the best we can hope for is amnesia. Thankfully Magrit has amnesia by the bucketload. She constantly rewrites her own past so she can live with herself in the present. This would appear to be her sole qualification for the job as local MP.

Magrit also accused Alicsammin of being the only person who posed a threat to the Barnett Formula just a few short weeks after she herself said it ought to be scrapped. She claimed she "wasn't around" back when the Labour government of Wilson and Healey deliberately mislead Scotland on the true worth of North Sea oil, yet at the time she was in fact the heid bummer of Glasgow University Labour club and constantly name-dropping her close association with Labour's senior figures and hobbing with Labour's nobs.

During the independence referendum campaign, Magrit expended considerable time and energy - far more time and energy than she's ever devoted to the interests of her constituents - telling anyone who would listen that if Scotland became independent her son in London would become a foreigner to her. Admittedly, "anyone who would listen" consisted of the Daily Record and much of the Scottish media, but that's simply another illustration of the problem Scotland faces. None of the outlets which were so very keen to publish Magrit's opinings on the foreignness of her adult son have been very keen to question her on her statement on fracking. But then that's scarcely surprising as Magrit's statement about her son being furren was of course complete and utter bollocks, as in the event of independence Magrit's Scottish born son would still be a

Scottish citizen even if he lived in outer space. And it would appear to be in the vacuum of the space between her ears that Magrit forms her opinions.

Of course, even if it were the case that Magrit's offspring would have a different citizenship and a different passport from her in the event of Scottish independence and so she'd be alienated from them and unable to love them just the same, this is not an argument against Scottish independence. It's an argument that Magrit is sorely in need of psychotherapy and counselling. Or more likely it's an illustration of the fact that Magrit will utter any auld pish that she thinks bolsters her position without considering whether it's logically rigorous, or indeed true. Which is another way of saying that she takes the rest of us for mugs.

Magrit is Labour royalty, and like members of the royal family suffers from sycophancy syndrome, which is what happens when a person of somewhat lower than average intelligence spends their adult life surrounded by Labour party hacks, and lackeys. Or in the case of Prince Charles, posh inbred dummies with long titles, and lackeys. Labour in Scotland is now also seriously at risk of inbreeding, as there are now too few of them to ensure enough variety in their rapidly evaporating gene pool. This is why Labour did not reveal the number of members who voted in their recent branch manager election - because the number is embarrassingly small.

Being patronised by Magrit Curran is like being lectured by a person who thinks they are an expert on the work of Steven Hawking because they read the star signs column in the Daily Record. But don't expect that organ to investigate Magrit's problems with accuracy, the paper is happy to inform its readers that Labour voted for a moratorium on fracking. But then the Daily Record thinks that fracking is a sexual activity indulged in by Tory MPs with orange segments and fishnet tights. Labour's against that sort of thing, but only because they don't get an invite to the party, and the Daily Record is against it, but only because it gives them an excuse to publish outraged editorials.

What galls me the most about Magrit Curran is that this creature supposedly represents me in the Westminster Parliament. The only person Magrit has ever knowingly represented is herself. Tell lies all the time, and no one believes you even when you tell the truth. With Magrit the trust deficiency has got so bad that if she had a pet dog she'd have to get someone else to call it for its dinner.

There are only 100 days until the General Election. 100 days left for Magrit's political career. 100 more days of expenses claims. 100 more days of lying and being patronised. 100 more days of the Daily Record not noticing. I hope they enjoy them while they last, because the clock is ticking and the countdown has begun.

I told myself when I gave up the fags that I could have a cigar on a special occasion. There's not been one yet, but when Magrit's career gets well and truly fracked by the electorate of Glasgow East in May, I'll puff away on a big fat cigar in celebration. Frack you Magrit.

Vow Academy, the Sequel

3 February 2015

There's really no need for anyone to be confused about Labour's stance on devolution, it's really quite simple. During the early part of the referendum campaign Labour wasn't going to offer Scotland any more devolution because it was a simple Yes or No question and Scotland could like what it had or lump it.

During the latter part of the referendum campaign Labour vowed that Scotland was going to get a devo maxy home rule that was just a baw hair short of full frontal federalism. You may have thought this was connected with a narrowing in the opinion polls and panic in the Unionist camp as they thought that Scotland was going for the 'lump it' option, but if that was the case your mind was clearly being warped by non-approved sources of information, like facts and things.

Following the referendum and the squeaky bum No vote, Labour tried to remove as many powers as possible from the Vow without collapsing it entirely, or more accurately by trying to ensure that its collapse could be blamed on someone else. The Labour Accounting Unit if Scotland spent their time during the Smith Commission consultation process playing devolution jenga. This wasn't actually that difficult, as the Vow consisted of highly non-specific promises to begin with. Even so, Labour made sure that Scotland wouldn't have control of the minimum wage or most benefits. You'll have had yer devomax then, said Labour smugurphly, and added that these were the very bestest extra powers it was possible to have. And something about pooling and sharing, which was mentioned every couple of minutes as it's clearly important for Jim Murphy's expenses claims. That's a vow fulfilled and we'll be having no more of that separatist nonsense as it upsets Magrit Curran and Wee Wullie Bain.

Now however the very bestest possible devo maxiest turns out not to be the very bestest or the most maxiest after all, because on Monday Jim Murphy - and some superannuated geezer called Gordie - vowed that if Scotland votes Labour in May we'll be in for super devo double plus good. It was not explained why this new offer of a super devo gob stopper that we can sook on for years without it ever losing its flavour was presented by a back bench MP who has already announced that he will be stepping down from the Parliament he's scarcely attended for the past few years. Neither was it explained why we are supposed to be reassured about the worth of this new vow when the self-same ex-politician who promised to supervise the last vow now doesn't think that the last vow delivers anything like enough. Gordie swore blind the last time that the Smith Commission was going to deliver "near federalism". So this time presumably Labour is going to deliver "almost right on top of federalism but not quite there yet, we just need to stop off at Celtic Park for some photo ops so Jim can pretend he's normal".

But Labour's attitude to Gordon Brown's political worth is similar to the attitude of the producers of the Police Academy movies to comedy. They'll keep dragging the old joke out even though we all stopped laughing years ago. In the next instalment, Vow Academy III, Gordon and Jim will suffer a series of supposedly hilarious misadventures as they try to ensure that the bumbling Captain Miliband is elected to the city council and will save their careers. Which also formed the plot line for Vow Academy I and II.

This new plotline, sorry offer, is entirely unconnected with any opinion polls you may have seen recently which show that more people believe that Elvis is alive and well and working in a chippie in Montrose than believe that Jim Murphy is an effective leader of Labour's North British Accounting Unit, or AU for short. In a supplementary question about the trustworthiness of party and accounting unit leaders, a large majority of those polled said that if they shook hands with Jim, the first thing they'd do afterwards would be to count their fingers. Or at least the offer is unconnected with the polls in the same way that Magrit Curran opposed fracking. The electorate have taken all this on board, and May's vote is looking like it's going to be a weapon of Mag's destruction.

By a happy coincidence, AU is also the generally accepted abbreviation for Astronomical Unit, the average distance between the Earth and the Sun. This is also a rough measure of the distance Labour has to make up in the opinion polls if it is to have any chance at all of overtaking the SNP and clinging on to its majority of Scotland's Westminster seats.

The promise of new improved all singing all dancing powers is Labour's master strategy to win back disaffected Labour voters by reminding them how much Labour has screwed them over in the past. It's a stroke of genius, or just a stroke. Certainly it's a product of brain death as Labour's neurones fail to fire. It's a clear and simple message which tells voters to vote Labour because Labour failed to meet their expectations the last time - but this time they really really mean it, pinky promise sure they do.

The new pretendy offer of new pretendy powers which Labour swore blind were not needed just a couple of months ago smacks of desperation, like a junky promising to give up the smack if we'll only give him a tenner for a wee bag of powers that's been cut with all sorts of rubbish.

Labour's upping of its devo offers is a lesson to the people of Scotland that if we keep voting ABLY (Anyone But Labour's Yobs) Labour will keep promising more and more in an effort to entice us back into the fold. And that's the thing about folds, it's where sheep are held before being slaughtered. So the offers are best ignored. It makes far more sense to vote SNP in May safe in the knowledge that the SNP will hold Labour's feet to the fire in order to get them to implement what Labour promised to implement anyway - and then some. Because we all know by now that if we vote Labour, Labour will only backtrack and deliver a tiny fraction of what they promised and will go back to treating the voters like sheep.

Pole-Axed by the Polls

5 February 2015

The Tory peer Lord Ashcroft has released his long awaited polls of individual constituencies and shows that the new clearances are about to commence. Labour will be turfed out of the croft and left with the ashes. It's almost as difficult for Labour to persuade Scottish voters to vote for it as it is for the BBC to find a clip from a 1970s episode of Top of the Pops that doesn't feature a sex abuser.

The results are - unbelievably - even worse for Labour than previously thought. And some of us had a very low opinion of them to begin with. On these figures, Labour would even lose Coatbridge. That's right, Coatbridge. For Labour to lose Coatbridge would be a humiliation like the US gold reserves at Fort Knox being robbed and cleared out by a 12 year old armed with a bent kirby grip. But there is more, there is schadenfreude with knobs on. Knobs like Anas Sarwar would lose the family seat that he inherited from his daddy, and Ian Davidson would be bayonetted out of his seat in Glasgow South West. News of which would set off rejoicing throughout the land as 1.6 million Yes voters cried out in unison "Ha Ha get it up ye." Because Ian has taught us all the meaning of the words vindictive, graceless, and crass.

Wee Dougie Alexander who is masterminding Labour's election campaign is going to have to mastermind a campaign to keep his own seat. This looks like being an even more difficult task than persuading voters in Scotland that Ed Miliband is not in fact made out of plasticine. Dougie's particular brand of skanktimonious pontification is proving as tasty to the voters of Paisley as a six month old unrefrigerated meat pie.

On a personal note, the best news of all is that Magrit Curran would also be turfed off her stairheid in Glasgow East. Writing in Labour List as the party dissected the dire news, Labour blogger Mark Ferguson wrote that Magrit was one of the "quiet heroes" of the referendum campaign - but that was only true because her screeches had reached such a high pitch that they could only be heard by bats.

On Wednesday the lovely Magrit tweeted from her stairheid, while she remains in possession of it, that the polls were difficult for Labour. Which is like saying that ebola makes you feel a bit peaky or that Attila the Hun occasionally displayed challenging behaviours.

The rapidly greying Mr Hi Jumpy was all over the telly screens on Wednesday telling anyone who would listen that the only people who would be pleased by these polls would be Davie Cameron and Osborne his pet iguana, desperately hoping that Scottish voters wouldn't remember that they could be pleased about the polls for an entirely different set of reasons. All Jim has in his defence is a tired auld excuse about keeping out the Tories - because that worked so well in 2010 when

Scotland voted Labour en masse and dismally failed to keep the Tories out of power. The truth is, as the truth always was, that the Tories will get into power if people vote Tory - and there's precious little that Scotland's voters can do to prevent people in other parts of the UK from voting Conservative if they see it as being in their interests to do so. But that's how it works in this better together union, the calls for solidarity only flow one way.

Jim, who's looking decreasingly smugurph with every passing day and every newly grey hair, is unable to offer Scots any positive reasons for voting Labour. For Jim it's enough to put on a Scotland fitba shirt and promise that Labour's the patriotic party. Like anyone is convinced by career politician Jim's patronising attempts to ingratiate himself with working class voters by making like he's a man of ra peepul as he mouths meaningless sound bites which are as devoid of content as he is devoid of principles. If Jim Murphy is a socialist, the Pope is the moderator of the Kirk's general assembly.

Labour in Scotland long ago shafted their principles more deeply than a fracking drill. All that's left is some noxious gas which bubbles to the surface every time Magrit, Anas or Jim open their gobs. The party has been hollowed out and cracked and fractured below the surface, in most of the supposedly rock solid Labour seats the constituency parties are moribund, consisting of a handful of local councillors and their relatives. Labour never had to contest these seats, they just took them for granted and weighed the Labour vote.

Now however the SNP has ten times or more the number of activists on the ground in Labour's safest seats. And these activists have, for the most part, not started to campaign. When the door chapping and the canvassing starts for real, Labour is going to find itself outnumbered, outclassed, and out of office. And this time they won't be able to bus in little helpers from south of the border, as they'll be too busy fighting their own campaigns. So despite Jim Murphy's fondly expressed hope that the polls will narrow as the election approaches, it's just as likely that Labour will plummet even further.

But it's not all bad news for Labour. Cheer up. It's really bad news for the Lib Dems too. The Lib Dem vote has expired, the air gone out it and it's shot across the room like a punctured Wullie Rennie balloon. It's about the only time you'll ever see the Lib Dems move purposefully, so make the most of it.

Danny Alexander, Osborne's little suppository, is set to lose his seat in Inverness by a huge margin. Having spent the past five years implementing cuts with an unseemly amount of enthusiasm, the voters in his constituency are set to axe Danny with the same glee. Danny is not only going to get beaten, he's going to get ground into dust by the very large rock he'll have to hide under for the rest of his life. And no one, with the possible exception of Danny's maw, will shed a tear for the passing of his political career.

Roll on May 7 - we cannae wait. Tick tock Jim, Wee Dougie, Magrit, Anas, Ian and the rest. Yer tea's oot.

A Stairheid Rammy wi Ma Mammy

13 February 2015

I've not been too well this past week, loaded with a bad cold while at the same time I've started a new part time job because I'm still not working for your other national newspaper. Meanwhile I am still battling the nasty side effects of the nasty medicine that I'm on for my nasty skin condition. So I've been too knackered to blog much. Give up smoking, they say. It's good for your health, they say. But since giving up smoking it's been one bloody thing after another. Anyway, onwards and upwards, or in the case of the Labour party in Scotland, backwards and into the gutter.

A few days ago a friend asked what it was that I have against Magrit Curran. "She's just a Labour hack like all the others," he remarked, "so why do you keep picking on her and not on some of the other equally obnoxious useless Labour MPs? After all, it's not like there's a shortage of them."

And this is very true. My friend has a point, we in Scotland are spoiled for choice when it comes to obnoxious and useless Labour MPs, Ian Davidson and Anas Sarwar spring to mind. There's the be-haloed Jim who has given the Scottish media the task of anthropomurphising the Labour party - trying to make

166

out that Jim Murphy is actually a real human being. But I do have a particular animus against Magrit, and will continue to do so until she is removed from office. I would prefer that she was hounded from office, preferably with actual hounds, but I'll settle for voting her out via the ballot box.

The reason for my animus is not because Magrit is a woman, although Magrit is fond of claiming that criticisms of her are motivated by sexism or misogyny. It is because Magrit supposedly represents me in Parliament, she's my local MP. I deserve better. Much better. And so do you. In fact I would have fewer problems with a chimpanzee as my MP because at least a chimpanzee knows how to screech and hoot in a meaningful manner. A chimpanzee picks fleas with purpose, whereas Magrit's politics are fleabitten and purposeless. However chimpanzees do throw poo and Magrit also throws poo, so it's not all bad.

In Magrit Curran, Glasgow East has an MP - a Labour MP remember, a member of the self-described "people's party" - who goes to £250 per head dinners at top hotels in London as a guest of US arms dealers, while her some of her constituents have to walk miles to a food bank in order to feed their kids. Magrit was a guest of US arms company Raytheon at the ADS annual defence dinner held at the Hilton Hotel in London last week, along with fellow Labour MPs Brian Donohoe and Gemma Doyle.

While Magrit was saying "Haw see us some mair o that free swally and duck a l'orange" some of the people she supposedly represents were looking at bare food cupboards and wondering how they were going to get through the week. Defence contractors don't care much about food banks, they care about schmoozing up to vain and not very bright MPs so that the vain and not very bright MPs will vote to allow the defence contractor to rake in millions. Few MPs are more vain than Magrit, and it's not like she's got anything much to be vain about. And she's as bright as a burned out bulb. Although, to be fair, that still makes her a whole lot brighter than the Labour MP for Coatbridge.

This week we got Magrit stuffing her gob in a cafe in Rutherglen where, between scones, she was extremely keen to tell anyone who would listen - that would mainly be the BBC - that Scotland needed to vote Labour in May because if we vote SNP then Labour might not be the largest party. She then added that the largest party gets to form the government of the UK. This is obviously the line thought up in Labour's line factory - or spin shop - or whatever they call it. It's also a lie. It is only the case that the largest party gets to form the government of the UK if the largest party also has an absolute majority of seats. Otherwise it's the party which can command a majority by dint of persuading other parties not to vote against it in a vote of confidence. You'd think that Westminster MPs would know this.

Magrit has previous for having a tangential relationship to the truth. As a result of her continual difficulties with actuality, her schmoozing with defence contractors, and generally being to political discourse as a monkey is to poo flinging, Magrit has been subject to some name calling on her Facebook page. Most of what she's been subjected to isn't big or witty or clever - but then neither is Magrit. Magrit has responded by attempting to introduce a new rule:

"Let's try a new rule here: if you wouldn't use the language with your mother in the room, don't post it on a public Facebook page."

This rule is not going to work though, because my mammy is also a voter in Glasgow East - and you should hear the language she uses to describe Magrit Curran. And my mammy is a respectable, intelligent and articulate woman who used to work as a teacher. Magrit would lose, and lose badly, in a stairheid rammy with my mammy. But that's what Magrit brings out in people - the invective.

The thing is, when you use politics as a vehicle for your personal ambitions and are bereft of anything that could reasonably be described as a principle, you're going to attract ire and bile in equal measure. When you habitually preach the most ludicrous half-truths and outright bilge you have no right to complain about others misusing language. Magrit's approach to politics is like doing a massive jobbie on the living room carpet and then complaining about the smell.

Magrit's can only claim to occupy the moral high ground by contrasting herself to people whose abuse of language is even worse than her own. That means the only folk she can feel superior to are trolls who yell swerry words at her. It's a bit like boasting you have one more brain cell than an amoeba. The Scottish media, in thrall as it is to the anthropomurphic tendencies of the

Labour party, will give her a platform upon which she can play the victim.

But the real victims are those of her constituents who have to walk miles to a food bank. The real victims are the men in those parts of Glasgow East who have a life expectancy lower than that in the Gaza Strip. The real victims are the hollow faced harrassed mothers who have to make a choice between feeding their weans or keeping the house warm while Magrit hobnobs with defence contractors and stuffs her gob with vol au vents and free swally.

Stay focussed, keep your eye on the prize, and let's work to get rid of her in May. Revenge is a dish best served with a ballot paper and a pencil, not a swerry word on a Facebook page.

Update: In the interests of fairness, and because I'm not Magrit Curran, I should point out that the Campaign Against the Arms Trade have now updated their original list to include a statement from Magrit that she did not attend the dinner event.

The Coyote Looks Down

18 February 2015

There's a country perched at the northern end of the island of Britain which is unnaturally blessed. You might even say it was blesséd with an accent and everything, because the diacritic makes it far more holy and so more appropriate that stories about it are illustrated with a photie of Jim Murphy with a halo. Behaloed pics of the Holy Jim are always in the Guardian every time there's a story about the Scottish Goverment being accused of something or other, which is pretty much every time that the paper carries a story about Scotland. However Scots don't feel that they live in a blesséd country. We certainly don't feel we live in a Lucky Country, a nickname purloined by Australians who make up for their lack of midgies by having hundreds of seriously poisonous wee beasties.

This made it all the more surprising that the Australian Labor party felt that it had to import Tony Blair's poisonous wee beastie John McTernan as its spin doctor. You'd have thought they had enough arse biting venomous spiders of their own, but apparently not. The experiment in importing noxious arachnids was not a success, and John's now back in Scotland spinning his poisonous webs for Jim Murphy. John's job is to cocoon Jim in a glossy silk of spin, a task in which he is ably assisted by Blair McDougall former chief tuba player for Better Together. Their task is to persuade Scottish voters that everything is rubbish, but will be marginally less rubbish if we vote Labour in May. So far, they're not having much success, even though Scottish people don't tend to think that their country is blesséd.

The average Scottish person feels that we live in the Wile E. Coyote of countries - all our plans are doomed to failure. We sally forward right over the cliff face of inflated expectations, we keep going even though there's no visible means of support - until we look down. Look down and then we plummet to the distant earth and our hopes disappear in a puff of dust.

However, on the midgie bitten cliff face of it, Scotland is even luckier than a winner of the national lottery. By any objective standard, Scotland has won the lottery of nations. It's a country which has even more energy resources than the Duracell bunny. We've got an embarrassment of the burny stuff that screws with the environment, yer coal, the oil, the gas and peat. We've got so much of it that the only argument Scotland needs against fracking is that it's just a tad greedy, like wanting to dig up the kitchen floor to get to a pack of stale digestives dropped down there by the builder when you've already got several packets of chocolate hobnobs in the cupboard.

We've also got windfarms on every hill, spinning in a productive and elegant manner, unlike John McTernan. We've got tidal resources, which once harnessed could provide the energy equivalent of the amount of gas it would take to inflate a balloon to the size of Jim Murphy's ego. The rich and civilised state of Denmark doesn't have all the energy resources that we do, although they do have the world's largest per capita population of pigs, a factoid which comes as a considerable surprise to citizens of the country with the world's largest per capita population of Labour MPs. Bacon allows a country to have a much higher standard of living and healthier citizens than Jim Murphy and a sea of oil. Which only goes to prove that Labour MPs are worse for your health than cholesterol.

But it's not just energy. Scotland has a diverse economy, an educated workforce, some of the best universities in the world. We have whisky. We have water in such abundance that we take it for granted. Scotland is green and fertile and isn't overpopulated. We've got a democratic tradition that is hundreds of years long, and although we complain of cooncil corruption, our corruption is minor league compared to that found in a former Soviet republic, or even in a Mediterranean monarchy. We're in a quiet and stable corner of the world, and have no border disputes or third parties who claim part of our country as their own.

The truly amazing thing is that over the course of the past 300 years the denizens of the Westminster Parliament and those in thrall to the Westminster system have taken this Scottish raw material, this set of conditions that is close to ideal for producing a rich, stable, and happy country, and given us what they keep telling us is a basket case incapable of looking after itself.

If Scotland is so poor, so inadequate - whose fault is that then?

It's not Scotland's. It's the Westminster political parties who are inadequate. It's not us it's them. We have political parties like Labour, which is incapable of opposition never mind government. Say what you like about Johann Lamont, but at least at times you could pity her. Jim Murphy provokes nothing but contempt. Labour lost an inadequate and incompetent branch office manager, and replaced her with one who is even worse.

Over the past few weeks since the party chose a supposed big hitter as its new Scottish accounting unit leader, it's suffered one embarrassing pratfall after another. Following from Magrit Curran's fracking of the truth, the Yes for Labour campaign that lasted all of 45 minutes, and the naked backfiring populism of being in favour of booze at fitba matches, comes the claim that NHS Scotland cancels four times as many operations as its English equivalent. Only to discover that the claim was based upon unequivalent figures. But it was all the SNP's fault for making Labour misunderstand the data. Anyway, Jim quickly removed the embarrassing tweets, so none of it really happened. Jim's good at rewriting the past, it's possibly his only real skill.

Labour is the Wile E. Coyote of politics and in September last year they ran off the electoral cliff. Now Murph E. Coyote is manufacturing one contentless policy wheeze after another, trying to disguise the fact that there is no solid ground. He's supported by nothing but the dust of John McTernan's media blitz as he frantically spins his way across the chasm. But on May 8, the coyote is going to have to look down, and we'll all watch it plummet. And laugh. That's all folks!

Making Magrit Sad

20 February 2015

She's at it again, but with just two pay cheques between now and an ignominious end to her undistinguished career as an expenses claimant, you've got to expect the lovely Magrit Curran to keep opening her gob in a desperate attempt to fend off the doom which is heading towards her career in politics like a mob of Transylvanian peasants bearing torches and pitchforks. Mags' latest is to inform us that we need to vote for her because if we don't it will make Davie Cameron secretly happy. It's wrong to do anything that makes a Tory secretly happy, especially Davie Cameron because he's smug enough as it is. So you should never attempt to bring secret joy to a Tory, except when it's also in Magrit's interests.

She was herself quite happy to make Davie happy all last year during the referendum campaign. When there was the prospect that Scotland might swan off to a Tory free future, Magrit waved a metaphorical and indeed literal Union Jack and cheered at the notion of Scotland continuing to suffer Tory governments that we didn't vote for. Davie Cameron was thrilled about that. He was in fact seen to smile, and indeed gloat. There may even have been a guffaw.

Thanks to the sterling efforts of Magrit and her buddies, Davie managed to avoid a shame-faced early end to his premiership and going down in history as the man who campaigned on the slogan Broken Britain, and who then actually broke it. Thanks to Magrit, Davie can still strut the world stage telling anyone who listened how the Queen purred. You can be pretty certain that Davie's job was not saved thanks to the efforts of any Conservatives, it was because of Labour. It was because of you, Magrit. Davie Cameron was oh so very happy about everything you did for him.

However none of that counted.

It doesn't count if Davie is going to be happy if it involves Magrit keeping her John Lewis list and travel expenses claims. Making Davie happy is only a bad thing if it involves giving Magrit her jotters. Still, she can use the jotters to tot up the amount she's claimed from public funds while she waits for an appointment at the job centre. It will give her something productive to do, which is more than she ever achieved in her career in parliament. But you can't blame Labour for putting her on the front bench - when she's up at the front they can keep an eye on her, because when Magrit's got your back she'll only stab it. Just ask Johann.

Magrit and her pals are determined to tell us that if we vote SNP in May, we'll get the Tories. It's the only selling point that Labour has got, but the logic is as dubious as Jim Murphy's commitment to socialism and as plausible as Ian Davidson winning an award for tact and diplomacy. Labour cannot escape the uncomfortable truth that

Scotland returned a massive majority of Labour MPs in 2010 - and in 1979, 1983, 1987, and 1992 - and we got the Tories anyway. If people in other parts of the UK are determined to vote Tory, we're going to get a Tory government.

The truth is that swapping seats between one set of MPs who claim to be against the Tories but not against their austerity politics, that would be Labour, and another set of MPs who really are anti-Tory, does not increase the chances of the Tories being able to command a majority of seats in the House of Commons. The number of seats which change hands between Labour and the SNP in Scotland has precisely zero effect on the number of seats which fall to the Conservatives in other parts of the UK, except of course in Magrit's imagination.

The MP who represented Glasgow East before Magrit was the SNP's John Mason, who took the seat in a by-election after the previous Labour incumbent - the unlamented David Marshall - resigned to spend more time with the proceeds of his expenses claims. Magrit Curran's election reduced the total number of SNP MPs by one, and yet we still got Davie Cameron as Prime Minister. She took her seat from a sitting SNP MP in 2010 and we still got the Tories in government, so you'd think that she ought to know that. Of course she knows it - but she'll still tell voters something else entirely. Magrit's very presence as a Labour MP gives the lie to the Labour line that voting SNP makes a Tory government more likely. That's Magrit and Labour's modus operandi, and that's why no one believes a word they say any more.

Labour tells us if we vote SNP we'll get the Tories. Meanwhile the Tories say if we vote SNP we'll get Labour. The Lib Dems say oh god please please please we're really sorry about everything it wasn't our fault. But's it's really quite simple. Vote SNP and get a block of MPs who will oppose the Tories while at the same time actually defending Scotland's interests. Now there would be a novelty.

I don't give a toss if it makes Davie Cameron laugh hysterically, although it's more likely that his hysterical laughter will be a symptom of an impending breakdown. I'm still going to vote SNP in May, and I'm not even an SNP supporter. I'd prefer to vote Green or SSP. But in May I will not only be voting SNP, I will be actively campaigning for them.

Meanwhile, I committed the tragic error of watching a bit of BBC's Question Time, a programme which bears the same relationship to an understanding of Scottish politics as nailing your scrotum to a plank with rusty nails does to foreplay. Never again, is all I will say, and I only watched a few minutes of it. Question Time all by itself demonstrates why Scotland needs a strong voice in Westminster, because we sure as hell don't have one just now. And there was us thinking that we were all better together and a happy family of nations in this sceptred isle.

Westminster's Francie and Josie

23 February 2015

Scotland had a wee visit on Friday from Davie the Pee Em, that's his new official title because he's dahn wiv da yoot. Being dahn wiv da yoot is also the same reason that Osborne got that new haircut, well, either that or it was drug induced. Mind you, it's not easy to say why leading Tories might want to get dahn wiv da yoot, what with the average age of a member of the Scottish Conservatives being 82. Although admittedly that's still a lot younger than Menzies Campbell.

Anyway, dimly aware that in Scotland politics is the new rock and roll, Davie tried to wow the audience out of their mid-afternoon nap with a taster from his new stand up routine. The funny bit, which wasn't funny for anyone at the sparsely attended conference, was when he proved yet again that Magrit Curran's relationship to the truth is similar to the role that black pudding deep fried in lard plays in vegan cookery.

Just a few days ago Magrit had claimed in an interview that Davie would be secretly happy for the SNP to take seats from Labour, whereas Davie in his speech to the Tory conference - or more accurately the outing from the residential care facility - made it perfectly plain that the only thing he despised more than representatives of a party which claimed to be Scottish, working class, and left wing were representatives of a party who really are Scottish, working class, and left wing. Davie was even more pure dead affrontit - to use political terminology Magrit can understand - that the wannabe pretendy Scottish left wingers and the actual Scottish left wingers might arrive at an understanding which would ensure that Davie was evicted from Number 10, even if his party did secure more seats than Magrit's.

Davie then attempted a joke. Or at least we must assume it was a joke. The Pee Em joshed that Labour and the SNP were planning a wedding, and were going to honeymoon in North Korea. No, I didn't get it either. You'd think that with the entire resources of the British state at his disposal that Davie might have been able to find a speech writer who understood the concept of a punchline. But apparently not. Not that it mattered with the geriatric audience, who laughed on cue, but then they probably think that Jim Davidson is a cutting edge satirist.

The truth of course is that Davie's real audience wasn't the handful of geriatrics in Perth, it was the voters south of the Border who have been fed a diet of scare stories about the evil English hating SNP. The Tories have already given up on Scotland.

The Tories in Scotland do have one useful purpose however - to prove that it is actually possible to be more delusional than the leadership of Labour's Scottish Accounting Unit. This was demonstrated yet again by former Tory list MSP Brian Monteith, the last cheerleader for Thatcher in Scotland, writing in the Scotsman on Monday. Brian, bless his little privatised socks, suffers from the quaint belief that the Conservatives in Scotland are standing on the edge of a breakthrough. And this would be true, in the same way that a cliff edge is a breakthrough in the landscape or the Gates of Hell is a breakthrough to Hades.

Brian believes that the voters in Scotland are on the verge of the collective realisation that Maggie Thatcher had it right all along, and we're just about to slap our foreheads as we work out that destroying Scotland's heavy industries and replacing them with mass unemployment and devastated communities while squandering the oil resources on tax cuts for the better off dahn sarf was what we'd always really wanted.

Meanwhile another blast from the Thatcher-past has got himself into a spot of bother. Former Tory Scottish Governor General Malkie Rifkind has received a malkie at the hands of Channel 4 reporters who caught him in a sting operation as they posed as representatives of a Chinese company. Malkie was caught on camera offering to use his influence for the company - for a fat fee of course. Malkie was pure dead affrontit that anyone should question or challenge the appropriateness of him seeking payment for lobbying work. It's perfectly within the rules, he bleated. Rules that him and his pals set up in the first place. Malkie was previously the chairman of the House of Commons Standards and Privileges Committee. Convenient that. A man who wouldn't recognise a conflict of interest if it was to jump up and bite him on the bum chaired the committee investigating possible conflicts of interest.

A man of his standing can hardly be expected to slum it on the measly £65,700 a year plus £116,000 in expenses that he gets for representing the citizens of SafeSeat in Toryshire in the House of Commons. A seat to which he decamped after making the realisation that money grubbing Tory careerists were unelectable in Scotland, where only money grubbing Labour careerists had any chance at all. Malcolm earns pin money to boost his modest income with an assortment of directorships and "consultancies" which bring him in over £240,000 a year. Clearly his job in the Commons doesn't keep him very busy.

Malkie told reporters on Monday that he deserved this extra income because of his skill set and his vast expertise in foreign affairs. This would be the expertise that led him while he was Defence Secretary in John Major's government to tell American senators Bob Dole and John McCain that "You Americans know nothing about the horrors of war" after they had urged the UK to support military action against the Serbian dictator and genocidal maniac Slobodan Milosovic. That would be the Bob Dole who was seriously injured by a German shell when he was fighting in the US army in WWII, and the John McCain who spent five years being tortured as a prisoner of war of the Vietcong.

But it's not all evil Tories. Former Labour Foreign Secretary Jack Straw is evil too. Jack has always been evil so this is of course news of the "It often rains in

Coatbridge" or "slamming your wullie in a door is as useful as voting Labour" variety. Actually that last one is not true, as if you are unfortunate - or stupid - enough to slam your wullie in a door, your screams of pain will be heard several miles away. Vote Labour and no one hears your pain - just ask anyone who lives in Magrit Curran's constituency. Jack Straw is a one-man conspiracy theory - just about any conspiracy you care to mention, and Jack's most likely involved in it somewhere. Nowadays he's taking his cue from Tony Blair, his former boss and spiritual mentor, and dedicating his charm and menace to making himself a lot more money.

Malkie and Jack are leading members of the House of Commons. Together this pair of chancers embody all that is wrong with that institution, and if Davie Cameron needed to understand why the voters of Scotland will be rejecting both his party and the Labour party in May this year, he need look no further than Westminster's very own Francie and Josie.

Big Lies and Wee Lies

25 February 2015

A Labour election leaflet dropped through the door yesterday, it's been popping through doors all over Scotland this week. It would appear that Jim Murphy's Accounting Unit wants us to vote for them in May's Westminster General Election in order to protect Scotland's NHS. On the interwebbies there's been a considerable amount of hoo and a great deal of ha about the identity of the nurse pictured on the leaflet, and whether she is in fact a nurse or is really a jobbing actress - or indeed whether she's really an ordinary carer and Labour party activist who isn't related to a former Lord Provost of Glasgow. Oh my God I'm a monstering cybernat.

Of course it could be that like Malkie Rifkind, who told us we'd be surprised at just how much free time he had from his full time job as an MP, the person in the leaflet was really working on the side as a highly paid advisor and is entitled to a standard of living commensurate with her status as an international statesperson. The truth is that it really doesn't matter, just like it really doesn't matter whether the other supposed member of the public pictured in the leaflet really is a mother with three weans or whether she'd never seen the kids before they were all hired by central casting and herded together for a photo shoot. Political parties are under no obligation to tell the truth in their election materials. They can use actors. They can tell you any auld guff that they like, and as long as it's not racist or abusive or an exhortation to break the law, there's nothing anyone can do about it.

Advertising standards do not apply to political material. Labour knows this, as they complained about the Tories' infamous "Labour isn't working" poster campaign in the 1979 General Election which showed a long dole queue - only it turned out that the people in the queue were actually Conservative party workers who'd taken off the pinstripes in order to pose as unemployed working class types.

Maybe the nurse isn't really a nurse. Maybe she really is a jobbing actress who's looking for that big break that will catapult her into stardom, in which case she's received an inordinate amount of attention just with a wee photo shoot for a Labour leaflet. Just like the Patronising Better Together Lady. That would be a small lie. However it is not beyond the bounds of possibility that amongst Labour's Scottish membership there is actually a nurse who shares the sentiments expressed in the leaflet and who would express them in a leaflet if it didn't mean that she might lose her job - because unlike Malkie Rifkind full time NHS staff aren't allowed to take on jobbing advisory roles willy-nilly. Much less are they allowed to pose in NHS uniforms and like Labour's Jack Straw take on advisory jobs supporting and aiding dictators from Kazakhstan for a very fat fee.

Mind you, it's getting less and less likely that Labour has any nurse members, as Labour's real membership has been plummeting and is now widely believed to be less than that of the Greens. And given the behaviour of Jack Straw and his erstwhile boss Tony Blair it is entirely possible that Labour now has stronger and more friendly connections with dictators in former Soviet Central Asian republics than they do with ordinary working class people in Scotland. Statistically speaking it's probable that Labour in Scotland has no members or supporters except Jim Murphy and his spinning staff and the news managers at Reporting Scotland. It is of course entirely coincidental that all this week Reporting Scotland has been banging on about the issues in Labour's election leaflet.

More likely it is quite possible that the Labour Party Accounting Unit in Scotland has a membership consisting entirely of Labour party elected representatives and their relatives. Jim Murphy regularly claims the party has a membership in Scotland of "about" 20,000. That would be "about" in the same sense that the distance between Glasgow and Edinburgh is "about" the same as the distance between the Earth and Pluto. It is when you compare both distances with the distance between Earth and a galaxy that's 13 billion light years away. It's all relative you see. So it's not that Jim is a liar, he's just a devotee of Albert Einstein. Honest. It will be on a Labour party leaflet soon. The other interesting thing about a galaxy that's 13 billion light years away is that what we see now is actually what happened in that galaxy 13 billion years ago and we have no way of knowing what is happening there at this present moment, nor indeed whether it still even exists. So very much like the Labour party in Scotland then.

Anyway, there's a far bigger lie lurking in the leaflet. Not so much lurking in it as hiding in full sight. And it's a big lie that risks being overlooked in the shock horror of cybernats monstering a working mum who may or may not really be a nurse. This is monstering in the sense of "pointing out that the Labour party is lying", of course. The big lie is the headline on the leaflet: "A plan to protect our NHS - 1000 more nurses, reduce cancer waiting times, £100m Frontline Fund targeting A&E". There is no plan, and there can be no plan. It's a big lie.

It makes no difference whether we elect one Labour MP in Scotland in May, or whether we elect 59. Health is a devolved matter, and how the NHS in Scotland is run is a matter for Holyrood, not Westminster. Labour MPs have no influence on how many nurses are employed by NHS Scotland, never mind the power to magic up 1000 more of them than whatever number has been promised by the SNP. Labour MPs can do nothing to reduce NHS waiting times, and neither can they provide a fund of a tenner - never mind £100 million - to target A&E waiting times.

But Labour is desperate for us to believe that its Scottish MPs can actually do something useful. In fact, their sole purpose is to act as lobby fodder for the party. That doesn't take up very much of their highly paid time, and so leaves plenty time left over for earning extra income from their second, third and fourth jobs. For all Ed

Miliband's sanctimonious hand wringing about ensuring that MPs only have one job, the job of representing their constituencies, the MP who made most in outside earnings over the past year was Ed's old boss. Gordie Broon topped the list of MPs with extra earnings, accruing £1,300,000 in the past year in extra-curricular activities. But you won't see that on a Labour party leaflet.

Vote SNP, Get Dettol

26 February 2015

E d Balls was in Edinburgh yesterday and together with Mr Hi Jumpy AKA Jim Smugurphy visited an engineering factory in Glasgow. The visit was mainly notable for its absence of anything of note, and as such was a perfect metaphor for the Labour party in Scotland. I've never been entirely clear why politicians visit factories, it's just one of the traditional things that they do. It's the only traditional thing that they have left when out on the campaign trail, now that they can't kiss babies in case they get mistaken for a 1970s BBC radio presenter.

Perhaps Jim and Ed, who'd changed his surname to Baws in an effort to blend in with the Glaswegian ambience, were visiting the factory in order to see what real jobs looked like since neither of them have ever had a proper job outside politics. Ed Baws wants to be the next chancellor of the exchequer, which means that if he's successful then the red briefcase traditionally waved before the press cameras at budget time will be a Bawsbag.

However it is just as likely that Baws and his Murphbag were hoping to discover a new manufacturing process for creating Labour voters out of discarded Barbie dolls.

Real live human beings have wised up to Labour, but the party does seem to have cornered the market in plastic airheads - at least if the braying backbenchers of SLAB and their cheerleaders in BBC Scotland are anything to go by.

In a desperate attempt to make out that the visit was more than just a photo opportunity for two not especially attractive men, the Guardian splashed with the story that Ed Balls had used the visit as an occasion to almost but not quite rule out the possibility of Labour going into a formal coalition with the SNP after the next Westminster election. This still failed to elevate the story from a non-story, since the SNP have already said that they would not enter into a formal coalition with Labour, but rather would support them on a "confidence and supply" basis as a minority government. Strangely the Guardian's ace Scottish correspondent forgot to mention this. Perhaps he doesn't know, since the Guardian's definition of unbiased when it comes to reporting Scottish politics appears to be "publish a Labour press release".

In the interests of clarification, this blog does not pretend to be unbiased. It wears its bias on its sleeve. Especially where Magrit Curran is concerned.

Of course the reason it's not mentioned is because Labour's strategy is to conflate a coalition with other forms of support, or indeed with the SNP holding a metaphorical gun to their heads. They need to do this so they don't scare off voters in England. Meanwhile they've already got enough problems with alienated

Scottish voters as it is. What's on offer is confidence and supply - which is more like holding a gun to Labour's head than it is getting into bed with them.

Confidence and supply is a peculiar turn of phrase, but then Westminster is a peculiar place. Confidence and supply does not mean that the SNP would supply confidence to Labour, although it might be interesting to watch Alicsammin try and boost Ed Miliband's self-esteem. Perhaps he might show Ed how to eat a bacon sandwich. What it means is that the SNP would not vote against Labour in a vote of confidence, that's the confidence bit, and would not oppose a Labour budget, that's the supply bit. This would allow a minority Labour government to continue in office, even though the Tories - who would also be short of an outright majority - might have more seats than Labour did.

Many sarf of the Border are outraged by this prospect. It means that England might not get the government it voted for, splutter assorted columnists - mainly on the right. Usually the spluttering is accompanied by a demand that Ed, the other one not the Balls one, rules out any coalition, alliance, pact, understanding, or breathing the same air as the SNP. Tories don't want Scottish voters to vote for the SNP, they'd much rather we vote Labour instead. Labour plays the same game as the Tories. So we get the Tories warning us that if we vote SNP we get Labour, whereas Labour trots out the old scare story that if we vote SNP we get the Tories.

Why Scottish voters should care about any of this is harder to understand, we've regularly had governments we didn't vote for. We get governments we didn't vote for all the time. And even when we do get the government we voted for we get one which has tailored its policies to attract Tory leaning voters in the rest of the UK. Ed and Jim know all about that. But that's what happens in this wonderful Union and aren't we all Better Together for it? If England does get a government it didn't vote for the response from Scotland can only be: welcome to our world, suck it up.

I don't know about you, but I'm getting pretty fed up of being told to vote Labour because people in England won't. It should be known to every politically literate person in Scotland by now, and thanks to the referendum campaign that's a large majority of the electorate, that it makes no difference how Scotland votes. We get the government that England votes for. This is not an Anglophobic point, simply an acknowledgement of the reality that England is far far bigger in terms of population than Scotland is. And in turn this means that if Labour can't get elected it means then it's the left in England that has a problem. Voters in Scotland can't fix that problem for them. We deserve better than to be the perpetual airbag that gets burst in England's frequent Tory car crashes where the only choice we're offered is to vote for the Red Tories in order to stop the Blue Tories. Don't dream, don't aspire. And for god's sake don't hope. Leave all that silliness behind, all that matters is that Labour gets to wave its Bawsbag in the Commons.

But the SNP is poisonous, it kills the germs of a Tory government stone dead. It kills the infection that keeps dragging Labour to the right. And this is all the more reason why Scottish voters are all the more inclined to vote for a party which will go through the lavatory of Westminster like a laxative and a gallon of bleach. Vote SNP get Labour? Vote SNP get Tory? The real political equation facing Scotland's voters in May is simple: Vote SNP, get Dettol.

Fossil Fools and Weasel Words

2 March 2015

There's an election looming, and the denizens of Westminster are doing their damnedest to make sure we notice them. This means that there's a flurry, or more precisely a slurry, of initiative and PR stunts which hope to make it look like the expenses claimants are actually doing something productive.

First up is Danny Alexander, who has as much chance of a future career in Westminster as the ginger dug - who isn't eligible to stand on account of not being human. Although to be fair, you could say that about Danny too. Anyway, Danny has now given us a reminder of all that he has achieved in his time as George Osborne's Parliamentary KY jelly. Danny's now arranged for wee plaques bearing a Union flag and the message "Provided by the UK Government: be grateful peasants" to be slapped onto infrastructure projects that are paid for by your taxes. Danny thinks that this will make people look more kindly upon him. Bless.

In years to come people will make a pilgrimage to look upon the marvels bequeathed to us by Danny Alexander. Gaze upon my mighty works, said Danny, and vote for me not that separatist person. Separatist persons can't give us what Danny gives us, for Danny has given us a union jack sticker on a broadband cable junction box at the side of the A882 between Thurso and Wick.

It's not exactly Ozymandias. It's not even Ozzie Osborne, who at least managed to bite off the head of a bat by mistake. Danny once bit the head off a jelly baby, although the general consensus of opinion is that Danny usually sucks.

Fossil fuel is the topic of a speech which Gordie Broon, Labour's very own fracked fossil fool, will make in Glasgow on Monday. Gordie is the diminishing resource upon which the Labour party pin most of their hopes. But he's about to run out, as after May he really will be an ex-politician as opposed to an ex-politician who's still claiming an MP's salary.

Not for Gordie the simple whacking of a sticker on a cable junction box. If it doesn't involve scaring pensioners, endogenous growth theory, or vows that no one will take responsibility for, then Gordie's not going to get out of bed. He rarely gets out of bed anyway. Even Malkie "You'd be amazed at how much spare time I have" Rifkind manages to put in more appearances at Westminster than Gordie does. And Malkie is the supermodel of Westminster who won't get out of bed for less than eight grand. Gordie's extracurricular earnings put even Malkie's in the shade - although all of Gordie's go to charidee. The charidee in question being "The Office of Gordon and Sarah Brown". So that makes it all OK then.

Gordie is expected to call for the oil fields to be nationalised, and will still manage to squeeze in the obligatory pensioner scare. That's the kind of thing that makes him a respected international stateman. Declining oil revenues mean that Scottish pensioners won't have their pensions paid, or something. Only Gordie has a plan to do something about it. Except he's retiring so he's not going to be able to do anything about it after all. And Eds Miliband and Baws don't show any sign of adopting it as Labour policy, so it's all totally irrelevant anyway.

There will be pages of analysis in the press, but the truth is it makes no difference what the superannuated has-been is promising this time. As long as Labour can put the fear of Gord into the over 65s, they might be able to rustle up a few votes. And that's all that really matters.

Afraid that the media hasn't noticed him for all of thirty minutes, after a few months of will he won't he, Jim Murphy has announced that he might just stand as MP for East Renfrew after all, or maybe he won't. Jim's still incapable of giving a straight answer to the question, instead he prefers to drop gnomic hints that are capable of just about any interpretation you care to put on them, and besides, the media will print any auld crap that him and John McTernan issue as a press release.

It's like his promise to end "exploitative zero hours contracts". The key word there is "exploitative". Any normal person might think that all zero hours contracts are exploitative, but the Labour party leadership are not normal people. They haven't told us how they're defining "exploitative". So if you thought that they'd made a promise to end zero hours contracts - contracts which Labour governments first introduced - you'd be sadly mistaken. It's not just workers on zero hours contracts who are being exploited here, it's the voters as well. Weasels and their words, eh.

Jim has been reduced to issuing press releases that say he may, or may not, stand for re-election in East Renfrew because Plan A has not come to fruition. Plan A apparently involved persuading a sitting MSP with a whopping great majority to take early retirement so that Jim could be parachuted into the seat, with the by-election to be held the same day as the Westminster General Election. This would allow Jim to sneak in under the radar without too much media attention on his re-election campaign.

Jim's cunning Plan A suffered from a number of fatal flaws. First it depended upon the noble proposition that a Labour MSP has no greater love for their party leader than they lay down their pension rights for a careerist on the make. This meant that Jim was relying on a Labour MSP to put Jim's interests before their own bank balance, because MSPs lose a large chunk of their pension rights if they stand down before the end of their term in office. So that was never going to happen.

The other flaw was that it relied upon there being a safe seat which could act as an inflatable mattress to cushion Jim's landing. With the Ashcroft polls showing that even Coatbridge is vulnerable to the rise of the SNP, there is no longer such a thing as a safe seat for Labour in Scotland. That just leaves Jim putting himself at the head of the Labour list for the West of Scotland region in the 2016 Holyrood elections.

In the meantime Jim still has to stand as the MP for East Renfrewshire, trying not to let on that he might very well stand down after a year. "Vote for me to be your MP for 12 months so that there is no break in my pension entitlements" is not exactly the most persuasive of election slogans. Jim's taking the voters for granted, but he's relying on securing the votes of all those Tories in his constituency. You can see why Tories would be comfortable voting for Jim, so he may scrape back into Westminster.

But still, there's the delicious prospect that he just might get beaten. That would leave the leader of the Scottish Accounting Unit electorally unaccountable. I can't decide which I'd prefer - to see Jim humiliated and out of office, or to see him re-elected as the leader of a Labour Accounting Unit that is down to a handful of MPs, and then to have to return to Westminster in ignominy, the leader of the red panda party. The only thing red about him will be his face, red with embarrassment.

No amount of fracked fossil fools is going to save Labour or the Lib Dems from their date with disgrace. 65 days, and counting down. Get the popcorn.

And I Mean That Most Sincerely

4 March 2015

On Tuesday we witnessed yet another dust raising policy announcement from the Murph E Coyote to disguise the fact he's run off the cliff and is frantically trying to gain purchase on thin air, and yet again it's a policy that's got bugger all to do with the powers of Westminster MPs. With no apparent sense of irony, or indeed shame, the Smugurph one announced that Labour is committed to keeping the Scottish Government's policy of opposition to university tuition fees. Jim appeared on the BBC talking about it in that soft voice of his - the one that is soft like quicksand into which principles disappear and vanish without trace. Jim's a wannabe Hughie Green of the 21st century, he's desperate to find a means of faking sincerity convincingly.

Labour's Accounting Unit branch manager prefaced his announcement with a note he said he'd been given by a wummin he met on the train, which - he claimed - telt him to shut it about the fitba and start doing his bloody job. I paraphrase of course. I'd like to slip Jim a note on the train telling him to stop making out that people slip him notes on the train, even Hughie Green didn't think his audience was that gullible. Hughie could teach Jim a thing or three about faking sincerity. Mind you, to be fair,

Hughie wore his right wing politics on his sleeve and never pretended he was a socialist. Opportunity isn't knocking at the door for Jim Murphy though, the sound he's hearing is a death rattle. And I mean that most sincerely.

This is probably as close to an acknowledgement that we're ever going to get that Jim's cunning plan to campaign for the right of fitba fans to get pished while singing the Sash as they smoke a fag beside a petrol pump in a hospital probably wasn't, on reflection, such a vote catcher after all. I'd say mature reflection there, but this is Labour we're talking about. They're mature in the same way that a three year old lump of dried up cheddar that's been crapped on by a scrofulous sewer rat is 'mature'. Sadly for Labour, the Scottish voting public are more likely to swallow the three year old lump of dried up cheddar than they are anything that's issued by McTernan's spin-department.

It was Labour of course who introduced student fees to begin with. Jim Murphy knows all about that as he was formerly the leader of the National Union of Students, and was instrumental in ensuring that the union's opposition to Labour's policy was muted. Which is another way of saying strangled at birth. Jim achieved this by means of "intolerant and dictatorial behaviour" - the words used by Labour MPs who voted for a Commons resolution to condemn Jim. For his pains, or rather for the pains of thousands of students who were left with debt, the arch-Blairite Jim - who didn't have to pay student fees or get lumbered with all that debt himself - was rewarded with a Labour candidacy.

We're still waiting for this supposedly "Scottish Labour" to come up with a policy which achieves two things - firstly to be relevant to the Westminster election and not the Holyrood ones we're not having yet, and secondly to differ from the equivalent policy espoused by Labour south of the border. If Labour in Scotland wants to establish itself as a party which really is a Scottish party, then it's up to them to prove it. Asserting it proves nothing. Earlier this week Jim Murphy asserted that he's not a Westminster politician. That would be the Jim who is a member of the Westminster Parliament where he is a representative of a UK political party. Fair enough Jim - now put your actions where that softly spoken gob of your is, and prove it. You could start by not standing for election in East Renfrew in May, and announce that you're going to seek election to Holyrood. Show some baws Jim, not milibaws.

But we all know he'll never do that. He's just going to keep on asserting things to a media that never examines his utterances critically, in the hope that if he keeps on saying it it will magically turn into the truth. He also hopes that the media won't highlight the potential get out clauses which are a notable feature of all Jim's commitments. He promised recently to abolish "exploitative zero hours contracts", but wasn't asked how exploitative was being defined. Normal people like you or me might imagine that zero hours contracts are exploitative by definition, but that's not likely to be the case with anthropomurphic types like the Labour party leadership. Which zero hours contracts would they not ban? We're not being told, and our media isn't asking.

It's the same with Tuesday's tuition fees announcement, as the Wings Over Scotland website pointed out, the announcement is silent on the question of student fees by the back door - a graduate tax.

The tuition fees announcement is yet another policy splash which has nothing to do with Westminster, it's a devolved matter. Labour's constant spewing of Holyrood policies in the run up to a Westminster election is not because the Labour leadership is ignorant about which powers are devolved and which remain with Westminster. Labour fought tooth and claw to ensure that as many powers as possible remained with Westminster, so you'd think they'd know what they were. Jim Murphy and his spinmeister John McTernan may be narrow nebbit, parochial, and just plain nasty, but they're not that stupid.

The reason we're seeing all these Holyrood policies is because Labour in Scotland can't produce any Westminster policies which are different from those of UK Labour, for all that they're trying to make out that they're more than just a branch office accounting unit which is entirely answerable to the twin heads of the Labour party - the Milibaws, which entirely coincidentally is also a unit of measurement for testosterone deficiency. All we've got is a pretend party led by a man who makes an oleaginous 1970s TV games show presenter seem like a model of sincerity. And I mean that most sincerely.

63 days until the clapometer gives its score for Jim.

The Fury of a Patient People

5 March 2015

Another batch of Ashcroft opinion polls in individual constituencies were released on Wednesday, and they could hardly have been worse for the Unionist parties. They were in fact so bad that even Reporting Scotland had to mention them, so that was pretty bad indeed.

The Smugurph was de-smugged as the softly spoken Jim was drowned in a tsunami of treacly goodness, although not good for Jim. Jim actually got off comparatively lightly, as the Ashcroft poll in his seat showed that he had a lead of 1%. This is well within the margin of error, so to all intents and purposes Jim's tied with the SNP - a remarkable fact in a seat which until recently had a Tory majority. It's even less comforting for him when you look at the raw polling data. Strip away the statistical conjuring employed by all polling companies to take account of previous voting behaviour, the gender, income and age of respondents, and what star sign they are, and you find that Jim was well behind. Just a tiny push more, and the Blairite who claims he's a socialist, the supporter of nuclear weapons who claims he's a disarmer, could lose his seat. That would be karma for the political chameleon.

Magrit's stairheid was rammyless and if you stood quiet and still you could hear the sound of distant sobs and neighbours complaining that she never took her turn with the mop, she just polluted the close with her sense of entitlement, so they've swept her away themselves. Wee Wullie Bain has run off back to his maw's, and Ian Davidson is wounded and limping away from the bayonet that's going to finish off his career in a few short weeks.

The big beast Gordie Broon saw the biggest beasting in his seat. In Kirkcaldy there's a projected swing of over 30% to the SNP, which will see Gordie's successor come far behind the SNP. People in Fife would quite like an MP who actually turns up and represents them. Now there would be a novelty. Kirkcaldy deserves an MP who realises that his job is to speak in the Commons on behalf of the people who voted for him, not to swan off and give highly paid speeches for a charidee that exists only to enable the MP to continue to swan off and give more highly paid speeches in expensive conference centres. Gordie Broon's the man of the people, the former leader of the people's party, who will only speak in front of vetted or paying audiences. He never saw the irony.

Over in Paisley Dougie Alexander desperately tried to take credit for keeping a hospital ward open in the hope that reflected credit might buy him a vote from some people who hadn't heard he'd played no part in the campaign to save the ward - he just turned up for the photie. Dougie's career is on life support and he needs all the help he can get. The Labour machine is going to be unplugged very soon, a visit to the Dignitas clinic is the only dignity they've got.

The Murph E Coyote keeps up with the spin as he leaves the cliff edge far behind. The McTernan Acme Policy Catalogue is raided for yet another cunning wheeze, but nothing works. All Jim has left is repeating the stale lie that the largest party forms the government and voting SNP reduces Labour's chances of being the largest party. That's not how the House of Commons works, and Jim knows that full well. He's just hoping that you, me, the woman on the 60 bus and the guy in the queue at the post office don't. But we know better. What do you do when the lies don't work anymore Jim? What do you do?

But the weeping and wailing and gnashing of wallies was not confined to Labour. The wallies of the Lib Dems discovered that they're even more screwed than Labour is, which is a bit like finding out that you're even less popular in auditions for Britain's Got Talent than a dysentery virus doing an impression of a zombie apocalypse. Although it must be said that Labour do an extremely convincing impression of a zombie apocalypse. Anyone who has actually seen Gordie Broon give one of his speeches knows just how good they are at that, which is probably why they're always by invitation only.

Charlie Kennedy made the realisation that he was going to have a lot more free time to muse over whether if he'd had given himself less free time while serving as an MP then perhaps he just might not have lost it. But it's even worse for fellow Lib Dem Robert Smith (no, I've never heard of him either) who some years ago was given a knighthood for services to being a nonentity. Boabie discovered that he's going to be paying a double price for his shortcomings. It's bad enough that he's a Lib Dem, and Lib Dems are now a byword for "lying scheming duplicitous gits who'll sell their soul for a ministerial motor", but Boabie also has a profile flatter than road kill and is about to turn into road kill himself. Sucking Boabie isn't just going to be beaten by the SNP, his vote share was lower than the Conservatives. That's like discovering that you're less welcome than Hannibal Lector turning up at a vegetarian dinner party with a recipe for home-made liver pate.

Not that the Tories have anything to crow about, down in the Borders Scotland's only Tory panda is staring extinction in the face. Davie Mundell, is tied with the SNP in his seat. Just a couple votes more for Emma Harper, and she can consign the panda to oblivion.

These polls are all the more remarkable for the simple reason that the campaigning hasn't even started yet. Even on generous estimates of party membership for the Unionist parties, the SNP all by itself can count on three or four times the entire combined total of members of Labour, the Scottish Tories and the Lib Dems. And that's assuming that Labour's supposed members are as motivated and energised as the SNPs, and that the Tories can supply enough zimmer frames to get their membership out of the care home. The SNP's members and activists have barely started chapping on doors yet.

So if you're a Yes voter and you live in David Mundell or Jim Smugurphy's constituency - or indeed anywhere else in Scotland - get out and get active. Support the candidate with the best chance of unseating your local unionist placeholder. Let's wipe the slate clean.

The English poet John Dryden once wrote: beware the fury of a patient man. Scotland has been patient far too long. The fury of a patient people is about to arrive.

Can You Smell the Fear?

8 March 2015

Can you smell the fear? It's reeking, rising in a fog of incomprehension, wafting up from the sweaty furrowed brows of Unionist politicians, dripping from the pens of the metrocommentariat columnists. It's the rank odour of a rotting and rancid Project Fear which is now eating itself, consumed in hubris, dissolving in its arrogance. Confused and lost by how events have turned against the winning side in the referendum. The wind has changed. It blows fair for Scotland.

It wasn't supposed to be like this. Better Together was supposed to mean that Scotland better listen passively, Scotland better do what it was told what was best for it. But Scotland isn't listening any more. We no longer listen to those who don't hear us. Scotland wants Home Rule. Scotland was promised Home Rule, we were vowed the closest thing to federalism it was possible to get. We were told that Scotland would have more self-government than any other devolved or autonomous administration. But we got control of road signs and unusable tax powers. So Scotland will use this election to take Home Rule.

The old rules of deference are dead, and we've learned that you get nowhere in this Union by being Miss Nice, by asking politely and patiently for things that the establishment refuses to recognise are ours. That's the lesson Scotland learned from the referendum. We're not asking nicely any more, and it's scaring them. An entire nation cannot be marginalised. There's more of us. They promised home rule, they didn't deliver. So we'll vote for parties which will take it from them.

Still the Union sails on, in a tide of sewage of its own making, of scandals and sleaze, child abuse and corruption. It promises tweaks, it tries to tack against the wind of change with a tattered sail of entitlement and a rudderless privilege. But the wind is sweeping it away, sweeping all before it. The life raft of their victory on 18 September is sinking, battered and broken by those who cannibalised it for their own ends. Ed Miliband and the Murph E Coyote are not waving from the stage of the Labour conference. They're drowning. The game is over, the game is lost. All that is left is to rescue what they can from the wreckage.

Labour stood with the Tories. Alistair Darling basked in the applause of the pensioned-off Thatcherites of Scotland. Johann Lamont railed against "something for nothing" and stood outside ASDA and grinned as a pal of Davie Cameron made threats to increase food prices. Jim Murphy drank Irn Bru on expenses and argued for Trident, for Iraq, for student fees, for privatisation. Labour stands exposed as the Frankenstein party of Tory policies dressed in a flayed dead skin of socialism that's peeled away to reveal rotting flesh and a cold dead heart.

Labour and the Tories both support the renewal of Trident. Both support illegal wars, both support demonising those on benefits, and in their poverty of spirit both sanction the poor. Both support privatisation, both worship the market, both bow down before the lords of the banks. Vote SNP get Tory, all it means is that the bully's wee pal is telling us to give him our pocket money instead.

John Major's old spin merchant Jonathan Haslam was on Sky News review of the papers on Saturday night. He doesn't know what more "we" can give "them". You and me, we're not "us". We're them, we're another, we're quasi-foreigners already within this happy family of nations. The old spinner for the Tories expresses the hope that "they" will come to their senses and vote for the Smurph. A man who spun for the Tories now wants Scotland to vote for the man who tells Scotland that he's all that stands between Scotland and the Tories.

Meanwhile his old boss writes in the Telegraph that the SNP can't be allowed to get near any power at Westminster, because, he says, they'll only seek to further the interests of their own party and boost Scotland, not the whole UK. Because the Tories have never done anything like that John, have they. The Conservatives have never sought to further the interests of their own party and to boost the Tory shires at the expense of everyone else. Scuse me while I do up the buttons at the back of ma heid.

But they keep spinning the nonsensical babble that is treated like sense by a media which lost all sense a long

211

time ago. Investing all their hopes in a gibbering gaggle of monkeys with typewriters, battering out gobbets of sound bites and incoherent policy initiatives, seeking a Shakespearean line that will resonate with an audience which is no longer watching the absurdist theatre. The audience is too busy writing a Scottish play of its own. One in which Glasgow East's Lady Macbeth doesn't make it past the first act, where she's sent back to her stairheid. We're writing a play in which Labour exits stage right, pursued by a Scottish bear.

Project Fear instilled fear, and created a Union defined by fear. Now it's being destroyed by fear. People forget arguments, they forget spin. But they don't forget how you made them feel. We remember the cannaes, the wullnaes, the dinnaes. We remember the smirks and the smugness, the condescension and the contempt. We remember the concert of scares and the orchestra of intimidation. Scotland has not forgotten, not forgiven. Now we're making the fear-mongers fearful.

We are the demons of their imagination, the spectres at the austerity feast. Scotland is the conscience that Westminster lost. There's an uprising in the kale-yaird. We're fed up with the over-boiled vegetables of Westminster, Scotland's planting exotic fruit, like the thought of home rule, the idea of sovereignty, the radical notion that in a democracy the political classes do what the people want. No wonder they are afraid of us.

The clock is ticking until the people have their say. And the people promise harsh words for those who spoke down from on high with words designed to cow and frighten. The levelling time approaches for the entitled ones. We're coming to get the Frankenstein party, pitchforks at the ready.

Bell End of the Union

9 March 2015

When it comes to Scotland, the Guardian's cartoonist Steve Bell is an uncomprehending humourless twank who long ago crossed the line between satire and a casual patronising racism. In his right on politically correct zeal to condemn everything he suspects may be nationalism, which is of course always bad when it's not of the invisible British Labour variety, he traduces and shows contempt for an entire country. Steve Bell swims in his Labourite British nationalist sense of superiority exactly like a homophobic UKIP oaf wondering why there are no heterosexual pride marches, and displays the same blank incomprehension of a phenomenon he doesn't understand yet which he feels threatened by.

As a result, the drawings of the left wing cartoonist scourge of Thatcherism would not look out of place in the Daily Mail. Actually, even the Daily Mail might pause and consider whether to publish them - their racist contempt is that obvious. It's sad and pathetic when a once loved cartoonist becomes an unfunny and abusive joke.

The alleged joke in the cartoon is that the core demands of the SNP are Scottish country dancing and incest. It's a ham fisted play on the quip attributed variously to Sir

Thomas Beecham, Oscar Wilde, or Winston Churchill: "Try anything once, except folk dancing and incest", which may have been mildly amusing sixty years ago. Somewhere, buried deep below multiple layers of condescension and offence Steve is trying to make the point that the SNP are so unprincipled that they will try anything once, including folk dancing and incest. But the joke falls as flat as Steve's chances of rescuing Jim Murphy's band of chancers from electoral oblivion. Because just about everyone in Scotland knows that the real unprincipled party is Steve's beloved Labour party.

Unforgivably for a cartoonist, the cartoon is poorly drawn. Steve seems to have got confused between Nicla Sturgeon and Susan Boyle. On top of that the cartoon is so poorly structured that the incest line seems to appear out of nowhere, tagged onto a tired old racist trope about kilts and Highland flings. There's no clear reference to the original quote, no setting up of expectations to be undermined later and so provoke a laugh.

So all that leaves for the reader is the feeling that we're meant to go ha ha it's pure dead funny because they're Scottish and have big hairy eyebrows and they're wearing kilts in SNP colours and that. Let's tag on a reference to child rape and fall about laughing. The only thing missing is a reference to sheep shagging - oh right, that's the Welsh isn't it. It's easy to get your racist stereotypes mixed up - they're all the same really those Celtic types. It's actually the deep fried Mars bar Buckie cocktail that we're missing. Here look at me, I'm a parody Scotchman being dour. I can say we're dooooomed, and there's been a murrrdurrr by a murrrdurrrurrr. Steve Bell

215

has murrrdurrred a jock joke before even having time to squeeze in a Krankie reference.

Still we should be grateful. At least this cartoon is remarkably light on the Jockanese language, the collection of misspellings and invented words which English cartoonists believe to represent Scots, containing words like "poond". Is that not the past tense of poon? I'm sure that's a sexual practice - come over here Stevie boay, and Ah'll poon ye.

I used to think Steve Bell was funny, and here I am giving him lessons in satire. Memo to Steve - satire doesn't mean yelling out "You wear kilts and shag yer maw!" Likewise, "You wear Victorian costumes and cover up child sex abuse!" is not cutting edge satire about the state of the Westminster parliamentary system, even though - unlike Steve's attempt at funny - it is actually true. However "Steve Bell is a snivelling cowardly middle class has-been that cannae draw Mohammed" probably is cutting edge satire. Not that I'd know, what with being a parody dour Scotchman. *Tu n'es pas Charlie, Steve, et tu n'es pas drôle.*

It's just a bit of witty banter, not racist at all. But those Scots can't take a jock joke. No sense of humour those Caledonians. Not like the English, who are happy to fall about laughing whenever a Scottish person makes a funny about their supposed stereotypical characteristics. No double standards there then. Not at all ... Oh ...

We've been here before. Before Ireland gained its independence, British newspapers were full of caricatures and cartoons which depicted the Irish as

216

something less than fully human - not unlike what Bell does with his Scottesque scrawls. The Irish were told they were improvident, incapable of looking after themselves and dependent upon the tender mercies of the Union to supply their needs or face penury and despair - just like the Scots are being told nowadays. The Irish were told it was unthinkable that their Home Rule advocating representatives could have any influence in the Westminster Parliament. Substitute Alicsammin for the Irish home-ruler John Redmond and this cartoon from 1910 could have been published this week.

The fury and bile originating from the UK media vastly outstrips in volume and quantity any anti-English sentiment found in Scotland. That's not to say there is no such thing as anti-English sentiment in Scotland, it does exist. But it's identified for what it is - an unacceptable prejudice. Anti-Scottish sentiment is dressed up as fair comment and is plastered all over mainstream UK newspapers.

But folk like Steve Bell need to spout their bile, because they are incapable of understanding the most simple basic fact underlying Scotland's entire campaign for home rule, for self-determination. And that fact is that it's not about England at all. It's about Scotland.

The Tory commentators and the Labour supporting Steve Bell - who is indistinguishable from them in this issue - find is easier to conceptualise being hated than then do being irrelevant. That's what really scares them - in Scotland in 2015, they are no longer relevant, and we no longer listen to them, we no longer define ourselves by them or their words. So instead they try to provoke a reaction by insults and abuse in a desperate attempt to cling onto their self-importance. And that's the real joke.

Getting Up from the Back of the Bus

11 March 2015

What do you call it when you throw a party and no one comes? You call it Labour's Scottish accounting unit. On the advice of folk like John McTernan, the leaders of the Labour party in Scotland threw social democracy down a privatised toilet in pursuit of a triangulated Tory jobbie, and now all that's left are the skid marks on Jim Murphy's Y-fronts. This is not an enticing prospect for any voter, and they're staying away in droves. Scotland has taken the claes peg off its nose, and has reached for the electoral dettol instead. It's guaranteed to kill 99% of careerists' careers stone dead.

The UK media has now woken up to the fact that the electorate of Scotland has collectively decided that it won't be laundering Labour's soiled pants any longer, and has reacted with a hysterical panic which isn't just borderline racist. It has long since crossed that border and is deep into kitsch kilt tinfoil glengarry territory. You could seek an explanation from the Guardian's cartoonist and specialist in Uncle Tammery, Steve Bell, but that wouldn't help much because he thinks denial is a tributary of declyde.

It's predictable that supporters of invisible British nationalism of the Labour party variety might be appalled by their party's impending annihilation, but the Conservative media is equally outraged. However it's not that Tory leaning newspapers are disgusted and appalled that the Labour party is in deep trouble. Causing deep trouble for Labour the sort of thing that Tory leaning newspapers strive for.

What they're really upset about is that Labour is in such deep trouble that they now have the same electoral prospects as the Scottish Conservatives. The only consolation for both Labour and the Tories is that their chances of re-election are marginally better than Danny Alexander's, although not by much. The real disgust of the Unionist media is that Scotland has turned its back on all the Unionist parties, and is seeking to have a distinctive voice of its own in the next Westminster Parliament.

This is, apparently, a very bad thing as it portends rampaging hordes of ginger rodents, Nicola doing an impression of Mylie's wrecking ball, and foaming rivers of blood. It's all got terribly biblical all of a sudden. Apart from Nicola on her Mylieball. The worst thing of all is that the UK is relying on Ed Miliband and Davie Cameron to do a Moses routine and lead the Union out of the wilderness and part the rising wild waters of the red sea of Scottish anger.

So much for love-bombing and telling us how the UK needed a Scottish voice in it. I seem to recall that just a few short months ago we were being told that Britain just wouldn't be Britain unless it had a Scotland in it. Our colourful kiltish characteristics and folk dances were an integral part of this Island Story, or at least of Steve Bell's cartoons in the Guardian. They needed us, they loved us. Please please don't go. Now however what we discover is that what they meant was - shut up, don't get up out of your seat at the back of the bus, and you may get some cereal shortly.

But the passengers have already got out of their seats at the back of Labour's Scotland battlebus and are advancing down the aisle intent on wresting the steering wheel from Jim Murphy's hands. The only question remaining is just how much of an electoral kicking the party is going to get.

Writing in his blog this week, Eric Joyce had some sage advice for Labour in Scotland. That's how low Labour has fallen. A disgraced MP with a propensity to alcohol fuelled violence is now their moral conscience. Eric believes that the only hope for Labour in Scotland is for it to become a real Scottish Labour Party, and to argue for the continuance of Scotland within the UK from the perspective of a truly Scottish social democratic party which is independent of Labour south of the border. But, he adds, even that is only going to be possible if Jim Murphy's band of placepersons, careerists, and dinosaurs manage to cling on to at least a couple of dozen seats in May's election. To be reduced to two dozen seats would represent a massive historic defeat for Labour in Scotland, but the polls suggest that even that seems to be hopelessly optimistic.

Eric thinks that if the polling figures are borne out, and Labour is reduced to a rump of less than 20 seats - and many polls point to Labour's seat tally being down in single figures - the, he says, the game is a bogey for the Unionist parties. Labour's only hope would be to reinvent itself entirely as a Scottish party advocating full home rule or independence - taking the party back to its historic roots. Because that's what Labour stood for when it was founded over 100 years ago. Labour then wanted to see Scotland with Home Rule, to have a similar status to Canada or Australia, self-governing dominions of the crown. It's taken over 100 years of the failed experiment of the British Parliamentary Road to Socialism to bring Labour back to where it began.

Meanwhile today saw the release of the GERS figures, for government expenditure and revenues in Scotland. There's been the usual smugness from the usual suspects, who are hoping somehow that a poor set of figures will make Scottish voters keep quiet and still at the back of the bus. I've said this before, but it's worth repeating. Let's take the Unionist crowing at face value. Scotland runs a massive deficit and has a dangerously unbalanced economy which is over-dependent on the plummeting price of oil. Oh my god we're a basket case, and only the tender mercies of Westminster save us from penury.

However to claim that this is an argument against full fiscal autonomy or independence overlooks the pointing finger. The Scotland with its massive energy resources, both fossil and renewable, its fertile land, its copious rainfall which means that the Scots word for drought refers not to a shortage of water but to the desire to have a wee dram, its abundance of food supplies, its highly educated populace, its diverse industries, its tourism, its world class universities, its ancient democratic traditions, its situation in a quiet and geopolitically stable and peaceful part of the globe. That Scotland. That Scotland is too poor and helpless to govern itself, too poor even to have devo max and fiscal autonomy within the UK. So whose fault is it that that Scotland is in such a lamentable financial state? Oh yeah - that would be Westminster and the Unionist parties who took what were the raw materials for one of the most successful nations on the planet and turned it into a feckless basket case. And they want us to reward them for that.

Let's get up from our seats at the back of the bus. Let's whack the bus driver over the head with a packet of cereal, and let's start having some influence about the direction of the journey we are on. Let's keep scaring the columnists in the UK media. Because when we scare them, they pay attention.

There's only one way to do that, and it's not by voting Labour.

The Ministry of Don't

13 March 2015

In this most perfect union, this happiest family of nations, this greatest political achievement the multiverse has ever witnessed, Scotland has - we are told - the most powers and widest influence of any devolved nation or region anywhere on the globe. This is only true if there are no other self-governing non-independent nations anywhere on the globe. This is not actually a lie in Westminster's weaseling words, as it's true that there are no other devolved nations. Other countries don't devolve power, they grant statutes of autonomy or have constitutions which spell out the divisions of power between states or cantons and federal governments. Only the UK has devolution.

Devolution is a term invented in the 1970s, referring to the loaning of power from the Westminster government. A power devolved is a power retained - and it's not retained by the likes of you or me. Like a yo-yo on a string, devolved powers can be wheeched back whenever Westminster feels like it. So the claims of the Unionist parties are true, it is no lie. That's the power of spin. Scotland really is at the spinning end of the world's biggest devolved yo-yo, but don't kid yourself on that we're holding the string.

The strings are pulled elsewhere, as revealed in an article in today's Herald newspaper. The real decisions about what powers the Scottish parliament should have are not made by the Scottish people, they are made by the mandarins of Westminster, the officials of the Ministry of Don't and the Department of Ye Cannae. And that happens behind our backs even when our elected Unionist Lords and Masters have promised us the devo-max earth.

As part of the Smith Commission proposals, Scotland was promised control over Health and Safety legislation and the Crown Estates, but in secret machinations officials from MoD ensured that control over Health and Safety was removed from the final draft document, and Scotland's powers over the Crown Estates were fudged and watered down. The Ministry of Deceit was worried that Scotland might use some of its powers to pit the hems on leaky nuclear bases, to force those who say they're keeping us safe not to cause us harm. But that would never do, because the MoD is charged with keeping Scotland safe and secure, and reserves the right to kill us in the process. And don't you Jocks go imagining you have any say in the matter - what do you think this is, a democracy? The only Jocks the MoD recognises are those under orders. Be regimented, there's a good stereotype, eat your porridge, do some Highland dancing, and don't be offended by jokes about incest. There's a seat at the back of the bus with your name on it.

The yo-yo spins, the elastic twangs. Scotland doesn't get the promised powers, but a glancing blow to the head.

There is no devo max earth but we do get the stars. A stunned and staggering Scotland seeing twinkling stars spinning around its head. Oh look at the pretty devolved lights, says the Daily Record. Marvel at the magnificence of your brain damage, commands the BBC. The yo-yo spins, the elastic twangs, the powers that were never there wheech back. Concussion is the vow fulfilled.

Scotland can't be trusted with its health or safety, we need the MoD for that. It's for the good of our health that the MoD needs to pollute our waters with radioactive waste. It's for our safety that they need to prevent Scotland controlling its own coastal resources. We might break something - like breaking the power of Westminster over our lives - and that would never do. Scotland the meek, the quiet, the subservient. It's health and safety. Just not our health or our safety. In the UK the health and safety of a Trident missile is far more important than your health or your children's safety. Don't go getting ideas above your station.

We've been here before. In the 1950s the mandarins of the Ministry of Delusion considered using the far north of Scotland as the site of the UK's nuclear weapons tests. After all, no one of any importance lived there, and they'd already polluted and island with anthrax. The only reason they didn't go ahead was because the weather was too unpredictable. In the 1980s the oil companies sought exploration licences for the Firth of Clyde, there was the promise of an oil boom off the West Coast. But the Ministry of Don't You Dare said no. It might interfere with their submarines and their weapons of mass destruction. We might discover that the Ministry of

Defecation was crapping filth all over our sea beds, contaminating our waters and polluting our seas - we might just demand that they stop using us as the toxic waste dump. They couldn't be having that. It was far better that the West coast of Scotland didn't get any boost to its economy to replace the industries that Thatcher was decimating.

The Ministry of Dengue Fever don't want us to realise that it's them we need defended from. They don't want us to know that they are a disease that stalks our country. But it's too late for that. We've woken up. We're conscious and alive. And we're angry. We're awake and we're dreaming of a country where our voices are heard, where our demands are met, where our governments do what we tell them to do. Openly, in front of us. No back doors, no secret meetings, no duplicity, no underhand dealings. And we're going to make sure that happens. The boys toys of the Ministry of Depredation will be put back in their box.

The Unionist parties say - trust us to lie to you, trust us to be deceitful, trust us to go behind your backs. Put your faith in the feckless, your confidence in the conmen. There will be a leaflet all about it put through your letterbox very soon, who needs power for the Scottish people when we can have hi-gloss paper instead?

It's been over sixty years since the Scottish National Convention, and they've still not given us what we want. Sixty years of asking nicely, sixty years of patience. My patience has run out.

It's time to take power back from them. It's time to break their power over us, to remind them who is the real power in this land. It's time to grab the yo-yo and pull it from their claws. It's Scotland's time, and that time is coming. 54 days until the Unionist parties' nuclear meltdown.

Dementia Opportunistica and Tittiferous Twankmonkeys

14 March 2015

I t was almost possible to feel sorry for Jim Murphy this week. Almost, but not quite. Fortunately, it was a whole lot easier to have a smirk and a spot of gloating as the Great Careerist's career tripped over a prittstick and came unstuck amidst a stickiness of glue puns. This is an embarrassment that's going to adhere to him for a good while to come.

The glue related merriment, for everyone but Jim that is, was all due to a question asked of the leaders of Scotland's main political parties during a debate at Glasgow University. And Wee Wullie Rennie was there as well. When asked if they'd ever taken drugs, three out of the four admitted that they'd toked a joint when they were young and shtupit. Because if you didn't smoke cannabis when you were young and daft then you've never been young and daft at all, and you are in fact a humourless party drone who's never had a life and has no business legislating for the rest of us, who still have lives.

Nicola, Ruth the Tory Action Krankie, and Wee Wullie all said they had partaken of a wee spliff. Although all were just as quick to assert that they didn't like it much and it had no effect on them. Which can only mean that they weren't doing it properly. You're supposed to inhale, and then you're supposed to traipse down Great Western Road at 3 am in search of fag papers and a curry shop that's still open, while saying things like: But like, wow, like if there's an infinite number of universes then that means there's a universe somewhere where Jim Murphy got a degree, but there still aren't any where he's got any principles.

But still, kudos for honesty. It's nice to discover that three of our leading politicians are actually human beings.

The only one who didn't admit to inhaling a magic rollie was the great doobie of the Labour party. This is almost certainly because Jim was as much fun to be around at university as he is now, so that must have been a pretty miserable nine years then, and he didn't even get a degree to make up for the lack of partay as opposed to party. But not to be outdone, Jim sort of hinted that he may have said Uhu to a spot of glue, because finding your jollies in a puddle of bostik at the bottom of a crisp poke is the sort of thing you're tempted to do when you sleep in a drawer on a council scheme. Jim's far too butch for giggly hippy drugs. Not for Jim an admission of effete middle class cannabis smoking in a student dorm. Oh no, Jim's far more authentically working class in the way that only an inveterate careerist can imagine.

Sadly, Jim was unable to adhere to the story and later admitted that he'd just stuck a crisp poke to his face with some blu-tac because he hoped that people might confuse him with Darth Vader and take him seriously. After all, he's already got the creepy voice and figured he was halfway there. But then he released a statement denying that he knew what PVA was, quickly followed by a statement saying that he couldn't remember exactly as he'd just been innocently blowing his nose on a copy of the self-help manual 'Fake Street Cred for Careerists On the Make' and it slipped up his nostrils. He didn't inhale. Or exhale. But whatever it was it was all the fault of the SNP. Jim had no way of knowing that you can make adhesives with egg white. Or something.

It remains unclear how it's possible not to remember whether you've ever sniffed glue. Unless sniffing glue has caused such dreadful brain damage that entire sections of your life are blank to you, in which case you'd probably remember that sniffing glue was the cause of your memory loss. Or at least your care assistant would be on hand to remind you to stick a post it note on your fridge, with glue, and that would bring the traumatic memories back.

Alternatively it's more likely that Jim is suffering from another type of memory loss - dementia opportunistica. This is a type of dementia which careerists on the make are sadly prone to. It's caused by an overweening sense of entitlement and a desire to rewrite the past in order to maximise expenses claims in the present. Symptoms include speaking softly to sympathetic BBC interviewers and appearing in backlit photies in the Guardian which make it look like you've got a halo on yer heid. The condition makes Jim forget that he's really a right wing advocate of privatisation, illegal wars, nuclear missiles and an opponent of further devolution. This can be the only explanation for Jim's current insistence that he's really a Scottish socialist politician who wants doublevowplusness. But that assertion is as plausible as Darth Vader with a crisp poke on his gob, and considerably creepier.

Meanwhile David Coburn, or as I call him, Davie the tittiferous twankmonkey, has got himself into a spot of bother. Oh sorry that was just a slip of the tongue. I really meant to say David Coburn the UKIP MEP and self-regarding self-abuser with the IQ of a mayfly and a political life expectancy that's not much longer. Easy mistake to make eh. Just about everyone and their granny has called on Davie to apologise, resign, and then tie himself into a sack and throw himself into the Forth and Clyde canal, but so far he's staunchly refused. Being bereft of any sense of shame, or indeed sentience, is a precondition for being a UKIP supporter in Scotland.

Anyway, japing Davie called Humza Yusaf, the SNP foreign affairs spokesperson with the Bambi eyes, by the name of a convicted terrorist because it was just a wee joke and they're both Muslim. It's the sort of joke that plays well to people who say they're not racist but who follow it with a but. As in - I'm not racist but ... I'm a UKIP MEP. Or even - I've got nothing personal against UKIP party balloons, but Davie Coburn is still a tittiferous twankmonkey.

Davie thinks that because his comments were made "off the record" then they don't count. Which clearly means that if you overhear someone calling you a dickhead, then you have no right to urinate in their beer when they leave their pint unattended in the pub. Davie better keep a very close eye on his pints in future then.

Not Joining Westminster's Gang

16 March 2015

According to the Guardian, the Labour party is close to ruling out entering into a formal coalition with the SNP should Labour fail to win an overall majority in May's General Election. Since the SNP have been shouting from the rooftops for months now that they have no intention of entering into a formal coalition with Labour, but would consider an informal arrangement not to bring down a minority Labour government, this is news of the non-news variety. It's a bit like the Gary Glitter Fan Club announcing that they will not, after all, be holding their Do You Wanna Be In My Gang membership drive at the head offices of the Girl Guides.

It's not clear why the British media persist in talking about a Labour coalition with the SNP when the SNP have already ruled it out. A formal Labour-SNP coalition is a decidedly Tory notion, one designed to scare English voters with the prospect of Alicsammin as a cabinet minister, although why this is a less appealing prospect than Iain Duncan Smith as a cabinet minister isn't clear. Mind you, having Vlad the Impaler as a cabinet minister is more appealing than having Iain Duncan Smith, and he'd be considerably more compassionate too. The strategy puts the focus on Labour, and is intended to deflect similarly difficult questions about possible Tory deals with the swivel eyed barrage balloons of UKIP.

However, because of this Tory election strategy, based upon demonising an entire constituent nation of the UK, Labour has come under intense pressure to rule out going into a coalition with the hairy bekilted barbarian country dancing hordes. After all, the forces of ceilidhdom lost the referendum. It's just not British to reward Scottish people for failure, or indeed for anything else. Who do they think they are? Bankers or financial service company directors? It is unconscionable that Scottish votes should count except of course when they can safely be added to the tallies of UK parties. Then Scottish votes don't count either, but in a different, and properly British, way.

So he doesn't feel left out, Nick Clegg has already ruled out doing any sort of deal with the SNP. But then this is Nick Clegg we're talking about here, and we all know just how much credence we can place in a Lib Dem pre-election pledge. About as much as you can in the Vow or just about anything that comes out of Gordon Brown's gob. However, it is true that Nick Clegg won't be doing any sort of a deal with the SNP after the election, or indeed anyone else, because Nick Clegg will have been flushed down the electoral toilet with the rest of the Lib Dems. We remember what happened the last time they made a pledge, and it ended in a ministerial motor and Danny Alexander inserting himself far up inside the rectum of austerity.

The notion that voters in Scotland are - to say the least - chuffed off that their votes do not count, and have decided to do something about it, has set the Westminster establishment in a panic not seen since the last time that Scottish voters scared the bejeezus out of them. That would be in September last year. That panic attack produced a Vow to introduce doubledevoplusmaxiness which was then traduced and watered down more than a homoeopathic remedy during the Smith Commission negotiations in which Labour, Tory and Lib Dem representatives spent most of their time on the phone to head office in London being told to gut and fillet the proposals like the wet fish with which Scottish voters are about to slap Labour across the face. So since the organ grinder's monkeys have not come through with the goods, the voters of Scotland have decided to take over the organ. The organ grinder is naturally not best pleased.

Anyway, the UK media has come over all pettit lip and pouty because it's dawned on them that a large contingent of SNP MPs at Westminster could hold the balance of power, and effectively choose which tune the Westminster organ gets to play in the next UK government. This means Scotland having an influence in choosing England's government, and that is what is setting the metrocommentariat in a tizzy. England not getting the government it votes for is an insult to democracy. Scotland not getting the government it votes for is just part and parcel of this wunnerful familee of nations that we're all better together in. Oh the irony.

The Tory media is furious about this, and there was us thinking that irony was a British characteristic.

Meanwhile the Guardian's political correspondent Andrew Rawnsley reports a conversation he had with a Scottish Labour MP he describes, in an interesting choice of words, as a "sane chap". Sanity is clearly something that's rare enough amongst Labour MPs from Scotland that it counts as a distinguishing feature. Despite having a majority of over 10,000, the MP realises that his seat has already been as good as lost to the SNP. The MP has accepted defeat, or to use his own words - "I'm fucked." Now he's just going through the motions so he can get his pension. Exactly how going through the motions so he can get his pension differs from what Labour MPs from Scotland do normally, Mr Rawnsley did not explain.

These MPs are as desperate for Miliband to state categorically that no deal will be done with the SNP as Davie Cameron is. Not the first time that the interests of Scotland's Labour MPs coincide with those of the Conservatives. The dead men and women walking of Labour are pinning their hopes, yet again, on limiting the choices of the Scottish electorate in the interests of personal advantage. But this time it's unlikely to work.

Under pressure from the Tories on one side, and its panic stricken Scottish MPs on the other, Labour will most likely announce soon that it rules out a formal deal with the SNP. However Labour can't, and won't, rule out reaching an informal deal with the SNP. Labour is attempting to dress this up in high sounding rhetoric - claiming that it's unfair to tell Scotland that Scottish votes don't count, and that it could bring about the end of the Union. Not that Labour was ever over bothered much in the past by Scottish electoral irrelevance. They now face the cold hard reality that without the support of the SNP they're likely to be as screwed as their Scottish MPs.

Scotland doesn't want to be in Westminster's gang any more, we've discovered we can crack the whip from a distance and make them dance to our tune for a change - and that's far more satisfying.

The Triangulation Dance

17 March 2015

Alicsammin's memoir of the referendum campaign is now in the shops, and it promises to be infinitely more readable than Alan Cockring's self-serving reminisces, although that's not difficult. The Japanese language instructions for setting up a Unix based server dedicated to accountancy programs and paint timing sequences are more readable than anything that issues from the poison pen of the Cockring. And a whole lot wittier. I mean seriously Alan, if you want to do a character assassination, attack a person's character - making snide references to personal appearance just doesn't cut it ya overweight beardie fashion disaster with a bad haircut.

Onieweys, according to Alicsammin, it was the Labour party which turned his dad into an SNP voter. Samminsenior's not alone there. The SNP looks like it's going to receive the votes of almost two million people on Scotland's electoral register and about 1,999,999 of them were turned into SNP voters by the Labour party. In Samminsenior's case, the conversion was achieved many years ago by a Labour canvasser possessed of the wit and charm of Alan Cockring, who referred to the SNP as the Scottish Nose Pickers. Samminsenior was so offended by the childish bile that he's voted SNP ever since.

For many of the rest of the almost two million, the conversion was also achieved by Labour bile and spite. It wasn't always as overtly childish as the Nose Pickers line, for many it was the Bain Principle. It was accidently revealed in some Labour emails by Glasgow MP Wee Wullie Ah Stey Wi Ma Maw Bain that the Parliamentary Labour party has a policy of not backing or supporting any SNP motion in the House of Commons - even if it's one that Labour does otherwise agree with. The fact it was put forward by the SNP is enough for Labour to act like the political equivalent of a nine year old school kid with a grudge against a more popular girl, although that's being terribly unfair to the emotional maturity of nine year olds. The SNP's just ugly, and it smells, and it's not all that. Who does it think it is eh?

There's only so much of it a sane grown up person can take before insisting that the biliousness one buggers off to its bedroom with no telly or mobile phone or tablet until it shuts up and learns the meaning of the phrase good grace. The SNP just has more friends than Labour does, and until Labour learns to accept that that's Labour's own fault, Labour will not succeed in winning any of its friends back. Now its left solely with the sympathy of people like the Tory Alan Cockring and John McTernan, who isn't actually a Tory but might as well be. By your friends shall ye be known, or some such 1940s homespun philosophy. Labour has some very unattractive friends.

Many modern SNP supporters have not altered their political principles. In this fact alone they are alienated from a Labour party which doesn't have any principles. They still believe in equality, fairness, and looking after the poor and the weak in society. Labour doesn't seem to believe in any of that any more. In an interview with the Guardian on Tuesday Labour's Rachel Reeves, the party's work and pensions spokesperson, said something worth quoting in full: "We are not the party of people on benefits. We don't want to be seen, and we're not, the party to represent those who are out of work. Labour are a party of working people, formed for and by working people."

So if you're unlucky enough to be out of work, Labour won't even pretend to represent you. This quote came in an article ostensibly about how Ms Reeves would implement measures to reduce dependency on foodbanks. But she's not going to do that by representing people who are out of work. She won't do it by listening to them and seeking to ensure that their voices are heard at the highest levels of government. Labour will merely look upon them charitably, after first having judged whether they are suitable recipients of charity.

That attitude is precisely why so many in Scotland have turned their backs on the Labour party. Labour has become the party of the haves, the party of those who jealously hold on to what they have themselves. Labour has become the party of those who, when asked to think about the future of their country, thought about the price of their car insurance and told themselves that they were merely being realistic and level headed. Labour is the party of those whose horizons stretch no further than the nearest shopping centre, whose aspirations go no higher than an economy flight to New York for a weekend's break. Labour's aspirations are those of a supersucker cylinder vacuum cleaner. Labour's vision is the vision of a designer specs store and its dreams are those of a mattress shop. Labour has no poetry in its soul. It has no soul. But we still do.

That's why hundreds of thousands of voters in this country have abandoned Labour. They have no nobility, nothing to be proud of, no hope, no future. Labour offers the same materialistic future as the Tories, where things only have value and worth if they can be denominated in pounds and pence. It dances in a triangulation dance with the Tories, calculated steps that take it ever rightwards, off the edge of our souls. So ordinary voters with love in the hearts and spirit in their songs say to the Labour party - triangulate my arse.

We don't want to be told that it's wrong to dream. We don't want to hear those who tell us there is no hope. We will not leave behind those who are worse off than ourselves and consign them to the charity of the uncharitable.

It's not so much that the SNP has won Scotland's heart - it's that Labour has lost it. And it's lost it for good.

Homophobes and LOL Kats

19 March 2015

This isn't going to be a particularly funny blog post, because homophobia isn't funny, but apparently the most significant thing that has happened in Scotland this week is that some anonymous and childish wee airse has been saying nasty homophobic things to Ruth Davidson on Twitter. I have no time for Ruth's immature politics, but homophobic abuse is never acceptable.

I'm much older than Ruthie, and can, unlike her, actually remember the damage that Thatcher did to Scottish communities and the gross homophobia which the Conservative party inflicted on LGBT people. As someone who came out as gay when Ruthie was still at primary school, or quite possibly before she was born, the Dug has been on the receiving end of homophobic abuse for many decades. And some of that abuse has been of the variety that left yer actual physical hurt, with bruising and contusions, not just hurt feelings. So I know all about homophobia. The Dug belongs to that generation of LGBT who taught folk like Ruth what homophobia is, how to combat it, and how to challenge it. You learn an awful lot about homophobia when you realise you're gay in Coatbridge in 1975. But this is 2015, and we live in a different Scotland now - a much better Scotland.

I suspect that Ruthie, like any well-adjusted gay or lesbian person, was not hurt and wounded by the comments on Twitter, she was just righteously angered by them. That's a good thing. Righteous anger is a healthy response to unhealthy attitudes - but that's not a lot of comfort when you have to deal with the unhealthy attitudes in the first place. Sometimes you just want to put your feet up and have a nice wee cuppa and laff at photies of LOL kats, because that's the cutting edge kind of sexual politics thing that your average gay or lesbian person likes to do of an evening. It's certainly the closest that anyone in the Tory party has ever got to advancing the cause of LGBT equality, but that's by the by. What you don't want is to have to cope with eejits whose sexual politics would make a caveman blush at their unevolved nature.

The fact that having homophobic things being said about you on Twitter by an anonymous twankmonkey wi a mooth that runs like diarrhoea and stinks even worse should provoke such a storm of outrage and newspaper headlines is a sign that Scotland has, by and large, grown up in its attitudes to LGBT people. Because it wasn't very long ago at all that those attitudes were mainstream and perfectly acceptable in polite society. It's a sign that Scotland now has a healthy response to those unhealthy attitudes - and that means that Scottish civil society is itself healthy and mature. This is a Very Good Thing, with the capital letters and everything. However just because Scotland is healthy and mature, on the whole, that doesn't mean that there are not occasional individuals who are pus filled plooks on the face of society.

But let's be honest here. The real reason that these comments received the attention and condemnation that they have is because they were made by a member of the SNP. There is random homophobia on Twitter all the time, most of which goes unnoticed by everyone except the targets. There are even homophobic LOL kats, but I've yet to see them being condemned in the BBC's Reporting Labour Scotland's regular aww-look-adda-cute-kitten spot. Ruth Davidson herself said that she often has to deal with homophobic comments.

But those comments don't get condemned in headlines in the newspapers or make the lead story on the telly news. The lesson is, clearly, if you happen to be a lesbian or gay person who is subject to abuse, just make sure that you're abused by an SNP member and then you'll have the media queueing up to take photies of you looking sad and oppressed.

The SNP now has around 100,000 members, making it a truly national party in the way that other political parties in Scotland cannot compare, and it's bound to include amongst that number some individuals whose sexual attitudes are regressive and backward looking. But what is important is not that such persons exist as SNP members, what is important is how the SNP responds when those individuals open their snide wee gobs. Or type their snide wee comments behind the anonymity of a Twitter user name.

Nicola Sturgeon immediately condemned the comments unreservedly and the SNP member in question was suspended from the party. That was the appropriate action, and it's to the SNP's credit that they acted so quickly and unequivocally. The SNP member concerned has now made an abject apology. Compare and contrast the refusal of UKIP to accept that their MEP Jibberjabber the Hutt had done anything wrong when he made his racist sub-Jim Davidsonoid "joke" about Humza Yousaf.

So this isn't really a media story about the evils of homophobia. It's really just another excuse to bash the SNP, and by association everyone who supports Scottish independence. Those who oppose Scottish self-determination have a vested interest in portraying Scotland as a backward province which is dependent upon the advanced graces of the UK to drag it kicking and screaming out of the 18th century. It's something we heard with regularity during the independence debate - the constant reminders that the SNP has Brian Souter as a funder, although no reminders that Souter's homophobic campaign was backed to the hilt by the Labour supporting Vow publishing Daily Record.

In that respect this story is a form scottophobia and is an attempt to insinuate - without saying so directly - that all independence supporters and the entire SNP are homophobes. And that pisses me off as much as the original homophobic comments did.

Little Yellow Minions and Wee Dougie's Delusions

20 March 2015

Danny Alexander's other boss, the Cleggy one not the Osborne one, is in Scotland today in a vain attempt to rally what troops the Lib Dems have got left, which basically consist of Wullie Rennie, the Orkney Koalamichael, and those half dozen or so Lib Dem cooncillors who have not yet committed ritual suicide by throwing themselves under the wheels of Clegg's election battle bus.

Nick made the bold statement that he discounted the polls which show the Lib Dems are facing almost total wipe out in Scotland, a statement which politicians always make in public when faced with impending doom. However, unlike the leader of Labour's Scottish Accounting Unit, who made the delusional claim that his party was going to increase the number of seats it holds at the General Wipe Out in May - sorry, General Election - the Cleggy one simply restricted himself to saying that people were going to be surprised by the number of seats that the Lib Dems held after the election, predicting that his party may not lose as many of its 11 seats as the polls forecast. This is a claim which is much easier to fulfil, as most people will be gobsmacked if the Lib Dems manage to hold onto as many as two seats. Danny Alexander, most assuredly, will not be amongst them.

On Thursday, looking exactly like a prisoner making a plea of mitigation before sentencing, Danny Alexander stood outside the Treasury brandishing what looked like a yellow Black and Decker case. The yellow case may have contained the tools used by the Lib Dems to drill into their skulls during coalition negotiations with the Tories and then extract that part of their brains where their social consciences formerly resided. Or possibly it was Danny's school lunch box, and contained a half-eaten austerity sandwich, his CV and a reference from George Osborne saying "best minion ever". Danny's going to need it because he will be looking for a new job very soon, having already been convicted in the court of public opinion and sentenced to vanish like a plook drowned in Clearasil. Whatever it was he was waving sheepishly before the cameras, it was yellow, plasticky, and deeply unconvincing, which is also a fairly accurate description of the person who was holding it.

Allegedly the box contained the Lib Dem's alternative budget, which bears the same relationship to the real budget as Jim Murphy's policy diarrhoea bears to socialism. Danny intended to present his fantasy budget to the House of Commons, despite being told off by the Speaker beforehand that he could do no such thing. Apparently the budget speeches in the House of Commons are not the place for making party political points - who knew? Certainly not Danny. Danny's words echoed round an almost empty Commons Chamber, a pointless charade in a venue dedicated to pointless charades. Even Nick Clegg was too embarrassed to remain longer than ten minutes - proving that he does have some slight sense of shame after all.

Danny's pathetic attempt to pretend that he'd have done everything differently might have had a modicum more credibility if he'd not spent the past five years enthusiastically out-Osborning Osborne, and giving every indication that he was enjoying himself in the process. However now that Danny is staring electoral annihilation in the nads he cut off and handed to the Tories on a plate, he's desperately trying to distance himself from the public perception of him as George Osborne's little yellow minion. The little minions in the animated movie are yellow too, but unlike Danny they're funny on purpose.

But no one is convinced by Danny's cunning stunt, Danny is the cut price Dracula in the Blood Bank, the Hammer Horror B-movie variety when they'd just got camp and were no longer scary. Danny and his party are just the supporting act to the main feature. The Lib Dems are merely a side-show, populated by freaks.

The main feature, for which Scotland is already stocking up on popcorn, is of course the impending doom of Jim Murphy's Accounting Unit. Earlier this week the other Alexander facing doom, the Wee Dougie one, mused that his party's demise was all the fault of people talking to one another on the interwebbies, and nothing to do with the fact that the Labour party is inhabited by, and a wholly owned subsidiary of, chancers, shysters, placepersons, balloons, doormats, Neanderthals, creatures who make even Danny Alexander look like he's got some moral fibre, and worse, much worse - Magrit Curran.

The last time Scotland gave Labour a kicking, in 2011, Labour solemnly vowed that it would learn and it would listen, and it made a similar vow the time before that too, back in 2007. Not a great deal happened except for an awful lot of blaming the SNP for everything up to and including increasing the threat of alien invasion and the end of civilisation. Then there's that other vow that Labour had a central role in just days before the independence referendum. By now it's clear to just about everyone in Scotland who has a functioning neo-cortex and who isn't an editorial writer for the Daily Record, that Labour's definition of "vow" is remarkably similar to that of a junkie who promises they going to change just before they steal your wallet and piss on your flower bed.

In Labour's case the drug of choice is political power, and since the party shows no signs of reforming itself, nor shows any signs of being capable of reforming itself, and indeed displays no concept that it understands what listening to the voters actually means, then the only solution is to force it to go cold turkey. If Labour won't change itself, then the voters will change Labour for it, because it clearly takes a voter to do a politician's job for them. We'll change Labour from a party of careerist politicians, into a party of ex-politicians who've lost their careers. And as a bonus, Danny Alexander and the Lib Dems will get locked into a little plastic yellow box, which will promptly be put in the shed, and forgotten about for the next three decades.

This Wasn't Supposed to Happen

22 March 2015

This wasn't supposed to happen. We were supposed to be quiescent and quiet little drones, grateful for the scraps we were tossed, eager for the bones we were given to gnaw on. We were supposed to be eating our cereal, silently, shamefaced, and grateful. We were not supposed to be where we are, riding on the crest of an avalanche that's wiping away a century of Labour's wasted opportunities. Riding on the lead wave of the deluge that's drowning the entrenched interests of Tory rule. Riding on the landslip that's erasing the Lib Dems forever. Riding on a landslide and laughing and joking, feeling alive and vital, noisy and loud, changing the world with conversations in the street, in the pub, with blog posts, tweets, and comments. Running, jumping and never standing still.

This wasn't supposed to happen. But it is happening and it feels so good. Liberating like coming out into the fresh air after being trapped in a lift on a hot summer's day with a pub bore with bad breath. Blindfolds are off and we're at the top of a Scottish mountain taking in the view - and this land is ours as far as the eye can see. No wonder the lairds are terrified. We're their nightmare, and we're awake. We're going to take their privilege from them. This land is our land, and we will be the masters in it.

The truth is we are unstoppable. The people of Scotland are a force of nature, an organic mass of ideas, a living pulsing interconnected network. We cannot be halted, we cannot be corralled. We will not be dictated to by the media, we will make our own. We will not go back into the shortbread tin, our spirit is too big.

The depression of the 19th of September did not last long. It was a brief pause for breath, a change of tack, not the end of the journey. It was a slap in the face that invigorated not castigated. Because it was a highly conditional No. It was not an absolute negative, a final say. It was the settled will of Scotland to say "not yet, not now". A No that said we'd give Westminster one last chance. A no that said we'd see if they fulfilled their vow. And now we know what happened to that. How now Brown's vow, discredited like the paper it was printed in. Pensioned off and vain like the man who created it.

The landslide that began its journey down the rock-face of Westminster's implacable opposition during last year's referendum campaign was not blocked or deflected by the No vote. It slides on, changing the face of the landscape, erasing old certainties, gouging out the old patterns, striving still for the shore. It's uncertain how the dust will settle, no one knows what the moving earth will reveal. All that we know is that the future is being written, right here, right now. And we are the makers of that story. We are the story, the active ingredients, the agents of change. We are the avalanche. We are the rocks in motion. We are the future and we are here now.

It's a story that's being written by ordinary people doing remarkable things. It's a story that's being written by people who refuse to accept the tales we are told by those who have held power. It's the story of a Scotland that refuses to accept that it cannot define itself.

What changed last summer was that the rock called Mary and the stone called Tam realised that the story of Scotland is their story, not the story of the rich and the powerful and the well connected. And they started to move, they started to tell their story. They connected. They refused to listen to those who tried to define their choices for them, to tell them how the story must end. They became the avalanche, they're moving still. And the story is still being written.

The avalanche didn't stop because the Westminster parties confused the willingness of a generous people to give them yet another chance with subservience. They mistook magnanimity of spirit for submission. They were given generosity and thought they had the PIN number to our bank accounts, their hands in our pockets, the keys to our hearts. They thought they'd be given permission to go back to their old games while we would watch passively, and accept the inevitability. They were wrong.

And now we are scaring them. They can see the strength of our determination. They can hear the rumble of distant voices that combine into the earthquake that will demolish their entitlement, that will rewrite their rules without them being in control. So they rant, they scream, they insult, they threaten. They write panicked editorials in the press. They draw cartoons that have no understanding or humour. They proffer little bribes, a few crumbs to the starving, a drop of brackish water to the thirsty. It always worked in the past, but it's not working now.

The old certainties are as dead as Magrit Curran's career. The old way of doing things has the credibility of Jim Murphy's spin and lies. The old structures are as risible as a speech by Wullie Rennie, and crumbling like a Labour safe seat. There is nowhere safe for them now. We are everywhere. We are Scotland.

We've learned how to feed ourselves. We've learned how to educate ourselves. We've learned how to articulate what we want. We've learned that we are the judges of what is best for us. We've learned that we have no need to beg. We are not asking nicely any more. We are going to take what is ours, and we will not be stopped. Scotland is angry. They don't like us when we're angry, because when we're angry we will get our way. And if they get in our way, we will remove them. The removal vans arrive on May 7th. They're going to be busy.

Black Armbands, Glue, and Sleepless Nights

23 March 2015

The Unionist party leaderships have the attitudes to Scotland which are typical of the less enlightened tourist to furren pairts. Nice country, shame about the locals. If only they could just drop all that silly nonsense and vote like England does, then everything would be just fine. This is the closest thing that the Labour leadership has to principles, and with this principle in mind, Labour has a plan to win the General Election and stem the haemorrhaging loss of redness to the SNP.

The plan is not a very good plan. It is in fact a rubbish plan. It is actually a plan that makes any reasonable person guffaw in derision. But then it's a plan that was most likely devised by John McTernan and Blair McDougall and approved by Jim Murphy, so what did you expect exactly? It is however all they've got. For once the plan doesn't involve making vowsies and pinkie promises that Labour has no intention of keeping, and for this small mercy we should be grateful.

It's just a pity that the plan doesn't involve anything except pouting, carping, and harking back to a mythical grudge in a past that only exists in the imagination of a Jim Murphy which, he told Andrew Brillopad on the BBC politics show on Sunday, he is too young to remember. This isn't really a new plan, since it's exactly what Labour has been doing without success for the past ten years, but as already pointed out, it's all they've got.

Incidentally, the past time in question was 1979, and according to Jim Murphy's Wiki page he was born in 1967, which means he was 12 years old when the grudgesome events took place. It's surprising that Jim can't remember. I can remember lots of things which happened when I was 12, but then I wasn't sniffing glue.

Anyway, back to the plan. In a desperate, if not to say pathetic, attempt to deflect criticism of Labour for cosying up to the Conservatives during the referendum campaign, for signing up wholesale to the austerity agenda, for privatisation, for PPI schemes, for abandoning Clause 4 and for demonising the poor, the plan is to tar the SNP with the Tartan Tory brush and blame them for ushering in a decade and a half of Thatcher in 1979 and the destruction of the mining industry. Back in 1979 the SNP voted against the then Labour government in a confidence motion, a government which in any event had only a few months left at best - but only after the self-same Labour party had betrayed its promise to create a Scottish Assembly by imposing the infamous 40% rule which ensured that dead people counted as No votes. Those of us who were at least 12 at the time can remember these things, at least those of us who weren't sniffing glue.

In a further attempt to rewrite history, Labour MPs are going to wear black armbands and lay a wreath saying

SNP RIP at the miners' memorial, because that will make us all forget that the only red thing left about Labour are the shamed faces of those who used to vote for them but will do so no more. And it will make us forget that the Labour leadership refused to back the miners during the strike of the mid 80s and betrayed them because that played well with the Tory press. We can remember these things because we weren't sniffing glue Jim. Labour wants to stem the SNP tide with a display of mourning, but they only thing they'll really be mourning is the death of their own careers.

Meanwhile, according to the Guardian over the weekend, a senior Labour figure fears "civil disobedience" if the SNP acquires "power over the English". Labour is terrified that the Scottish tail may wag the UK dog, because the only tail that's allowed to wag the UK dog is the financial sector in the City of London. It's unclear what form this civil disobedience may take, a mass letter writing campaign by Outraged of Tunbridge Wells to the Telegraph perhaps. People will leave sharply worded comments in the Guardian and will tsk and raise their eyebrows. The very fabric of British existence will be threatened.

It will not go unnoticed in Scotland that senior Labour, and Tory and Lib Dem, figures were quite happy for English votes to impose power over Scotland, but somehow when it happens the other way about it's a dreadful threat to the fabric of the Union and fundamentally undemocratic. And there was us thinking that we were valued and much loved partners in this greatest family of nations that the universe has ever seen. The obvious conclusion is that it's not really a Union that the leaders of the Unionist parties want, what they want is a tame wee Scottie dog which doesn't demand to sit at the table with the humans. Scotland's not a partner, it's a prize. They're in for a big shock then, because this wee Scottie dog not only snaps and bites, it will also piss and crap on the rug that passes for a British constitution. A rug under which all sorts of nastiness has been swept.

Alicsammin said over the weekend that Scotland can hold the balance of votes in Westminster after the next election, pointing out that if you hold the balance you hold the power. This was described as "terrifying" by Tory Defence Minister Anna Soubry, who said it like Scotland having access to any sort of power was a bad thing. They wanted us to stay in the Union, they threatened, they begged, they pleaded. Now we're staying and they're complaining that we might have the audacity to define our own role within it. They think that this Union is theirs, but if it is really a Union then it is ours as well. Now it's up to the Unionists to step up, to put their money where their mouths are. Unions mean compromises, and that means they must compromise too. They've not learned that lesson, they've spent too much time sniffing glue, so Scotland is going to have to teach it to them.

If we're terrifying the Tories that can only work in Scotland's favour. They're not terrified by Labour MPs. Let's give Anna sleepless nights. They want a Union? We'll show them what that means. The Tories and the Labour party will have plenty more sleepless nights in the five years ahead. Scotland is coming to Westminster, and it's angry.

Vote Labour, Vote Stupid, Vote Glue-Sniffer

24 March 2015

Ed Miliband was in Clydebank on Monday, speaking to what Labour calls a mass rally. Once upon a time, way back in the mythical age of fairy stories and magic wireless and inventing the NHS, Labour had mass rallies which involved a Labour leader addressing a cheering crowd of thousands who'd flock to hear him because the telly was in black and white and Jimmy Savile still had a career on the BBC. Nowadays Labour's definition of a mass rally is collecting the useless tubs of lard who sit for the party in the House of Commons into one room, calling on some obliging full colour TV cameras, and hoping that their combined inertia can be mistaken for weighty.

Ed was in evangelical mode, mostly because only divine intervention is going to save Labour in Scotland now. He was preaching to his small and rapidly diminishing flockette about the evils of the unholy alliance between the SNP and the Tories. This came as something of a surprise to the SNP, and indeed to the Tories, who are even less on speaking terms with one another than Labour is. And Labour has spent the past eight years sulking in its bedroom and refusing to talk to anyone, perfecting the pouty spoiled entitled brat school of politics. It's safe to say that Labour has that off pat by now, and has thoroughly mastered the art of spoiled entitlement, proving that the party is good for something after all.

As the little group huddled together, fearing just how flocked they are, the Labour adenoid told them how immensely upset he was that the SNP was diverting Labour from its historic mission to adopt Conservative policies wholesale so that UKIP voters in Essex will vote for it. The SNP is forcing the Labour party to act like a proper Labour party and preventing it from being just like the Tory party, he complained. Even worse, they're doing it on purpose, he thundered. Well, not thundered exactly, this is Ed Miliband. Instead he sounded like a kitten with a bad head cold which was annoyed that it couldn't reach its ball of wool.

Because of the nasty SNP, the only way Labour can get elected in Scotland is by being left wing. But because of the nasty Tories the only way Labour can get elected in England is by being right wing. Ed Balls has a right not to find George Osborne's budget objectionable, and the word of Gord tells him to announce to the press that he wouldn't change anything if he was in power.

However, in Scotland, Jim Murphy has to adopt an unconvincing socialist drag, like a creepier version of Dracula's minion trying to pretend that the Garibaldis he proffers to the voters do not contain actual flies. All Labour in Scotland has to offer is a graveyard of insects.

Ed thinks this is unfair, and Labour's current difficulties are not because Labour has spent the last twenty years in an ever rightwards triangulation dance with the

Thatcherite tendency of the UK press. It's all the fault of those horrible Scottish voters for getting pissed off and saying they're not going to put up with it any more. That's just unholy. Indeed, it's blasphemy. The job of Scotland's voters is not to think, not to expect anything, not to have any expectations. Their job is to shut up and vote for Magrit Curran and Jim Murphy, like a good little flock of Labour sheep.

In aid of this Labour has been putting another leaflet through people's doors. Another effort delivered by the postie because Labour doesn't have enough activists on the ground to do it for them. It boasts, amongst other things, that Labour is opposed to tuition fees, that it will ban "exploitative" zero hours contracts, forgetting to tell us that it was Labour which introduced tuition fees and zero hours contracts in the first place. They hope we don't remember. That's Labour for you, it's the party of glue sniffers with advanced dementia.

The leaflet repeats the lie that Labour clings to like a lifebelt - the lie that only the largest party in the Commons can form the government. But it's simple arithmetic - 323 is the size of a majority. So if Labour has 275 seats, the Tories 280, and the SNP 50, then the Tories can't form a government, because they can't come close to a majority. Labour could be a minority government reliant upon the kindness of the SNP. If Labour can't cope with simple arithmetic, then how can we expect them to cope with the more complex sums involved in budget calculations? Labour hopes we can't count. Vote Labour, vote stupid, vote glue sniffer.

Meanwhile, the sordid squirming can of worms of Labour local government has had its lid prised off again. In North Lanarkshire a Labour cooncillor is suing the party for allegedly damaging his name and reputation after he raised questions about a deal done by the council with a company run by the husband of Glasgow's Labour Lord Provost. The leader of North Lanarkshire council has admitted being a personal friend of the Lord Provost and her company director husband, but has denied that this friendship influenced the decision to award the company the contract.

It's all a depressingly familiar tale. Move along, nothing to see here ... and don't expect an in depth investigation on BBC Reporting Labour Scotland any time soon. We will instead be invited to sympathise with the emotional trauma that the stalwart Labour party members have all been put through.

The interesting point here is not so much that there are allegations of nefarious and underhand doings in a Labour cooncil - because that's pretty much a given with a Labour cooncil - it's that the Labour cooncillor doing the suing can't sue the Scottish Labour party because no such entity exists in law. It turns out that there is no such thing as the Scottish Labour party. He has to sue the Labour party headquarters in London.

The question is then, what exactly is it that Jim Murphy claims to lead? It turns out that he's the fictional leader of a fictional party, spouting fictional policies. How can a party that doesn't exist separately from Labour UK claim to have policies that are distinct from Labour UK? Is that even legal under electoral law? Quite probably it isn't. These are yet more questions that it is unlikely you'll see being investigated in depth on Reporting LabourScotland any time soon.

Caledonian Cahootment

26 March 2015

So have you cahooted with anyone recently? Labour says that if you vote SNP you're in cahoots with the Tories, meanwhile the Tories say that if you vote SNP you're in cahoots with Labour, while they themselves cahoot with UKIP. The only party no one is cahooting with is the Lib Dems, but that's only because it's difficult to conspire with a body which is already dead, and even Derek Ancora can't raise Danny Alexander's career from its well-deserved grave.

You may, oh simple minded Scottish person, think that you're voting SNP and are going to get the SNP, but in fact you'll really be voting for Labour and the Tories and UKIP all at the same time. The only party you won't be voting for when you vote SNP is the SNP. But also at the same time, it is dreadfully un-British of Scotland to vote for all those British parties simultaneously, and it's a sinister threat to the integrity of the YooKay.

Faced with the prospect of being kept out of office because of Scottish votes, the Tories are in a particularly sour faced mood, although it's not easy to tell the difference because being in a sour faced mood is the default condition of the Conservative party. According to assorted Tory spokesranters, it would be a disgracefully sinister subversion of democracy if they were prevented from forming the government because Scottish people won't vote for them. Scottish people haven't voted Tory for a generation, but that's never cramped the Tories' style until now. However that was because Scottish voters previously elected Labour MPs, who are a byword for uselessness. Look up Scottish Labour in a dictionary of political definitions and you'll find that Scottish Labour doesn't actually exist. It's hardly surprising that a fictitious party can't successfully resist the depredations of the very real malice of the Conservatives.

Faced with the prospect of a big group of SNP MPs giving them the finger, the Tories are purple faced with anger, making them indistinguishable from UKIP. The Tories have been unable to attain a majority in any general election since the 1990s, and the occupation of Scotland by an anti-Tory bloc doesn't make life any easier for them. No more Danny Alexanders to sook up to them, and no more a Labour party which will adopt Tory policies in an effort to make itself electable in Bedfordshire.

The Tories could end up being the largest single party in Westminster, yet still unable to form a government. They think this is unfair, everyone else thinks it's what they get for doing all they could to undermine the Lib Dem demand for proportional representation. They also did all they could to ensure that Scotland remained in the Union, and so ensured that the SNP remained a British political party. Now they're complaining that the SNP isn't sufficiently British for their tastes and warning voters in England that Ed Miliband is in Alicsammin's pocket. Like that's a bad thing. What happened to the love bombs and telling us that Scotland's voice was a valued and much loved addition to UK national life, eh? Suck it up Tory boys and girls, suck it up.

Meanwhile Labour is equally convinced that the SNP is conniving with the Tories to get people not to vote Labour. In an effort to shore up what little support they have left, Jim Murphy is now promising all sorts of goodies, which will apparently be paid for by taxing mansions in London, or something. Jim's real problem is that no one is listening to his guff any more. Whenever he appears on the telly, all anyone hears in that creepily soft spoken tone of his is blah blah blah patriotic Scot blah blah football blah irn bru blah blah.

It doesn't matter what Jim says anymore, because most people in Scotland are already convinced that if it comes out of Jim's gob, it must be a lie. Whereas for normal people, what they say is considered truthful until proven to be a lie, Jim's now crossed into that dangerous territory where those who've lost trust live - what he says is considered to be a lie unless there is overwhelming proof that it's not. When that happens to a politician, they really just need to acknowledge defeat and seek employment elsewhere. Fingers crossed that will be Jim's fate in May.

Labour's only real talent is the ability to inspire odium in such a wide and diverse range of people. Labour is the giant ego at the party, the one who thinks it's all about them. They seem unable to understand that SNP voters and Tories are perfectly capable of hating the Labour party for entirely different and unrelated reasons, so it has to be cahooting.

Labour's giant ego was on display in the House of Commons on Thursday, as Gordie Broon actually turned up for once - but only so he could give his last ever speech. Gordie thinks that everyone is in cahoots with everyone else, but whatever it is they're cahooting, none of it is Gordie's fault. Mainly however he was annoyed, not that Tory proposals for English votes for English laws threaten to make Scottish residents second class citizens, but worse, far worse, that they threaten to make Scottish MPs second class. Gordie would have few problems with the first of those propositions. He just wanted to put it on record that none of it has anything to do with him. Funnily enough, that vow he was supposed to be shepherding through the Westminster Parlie seems to have slipped his mind entirely. But then Gordie is in cahoots with his inflated sense of self-worth.

As a simple minded Scottish person, my wee brain can't quite comprehend all this rampant cahootment. All that is really coming across is that the UK media and establishment are shitting bricks at the prospect of Scotland's voters taking them at their word and believing them when they told us last year that they valued and loved our uniquely Caledonian take on all that is British. Being a cahootsy Caledonian conspirator, the British establishment crapping itself seems to me to be a good thing. So feck it - I'm just going to vote SNP anyway. It will get rid of Magrit Curran, and everything else is a delicious bonus prize.

Getting rid of my local Labour waste of space is the political principle I care most about anyway. Magrit's sole claim to fame is having a vegetable based plastic used for making fishing rods named after her. It's all that she'll be remembered for. Coincidentally it also explains a great deal about the demise of the Labour party in Scotland - the party has sunk so low in public esteem because it consists of vegetables on fishing expeditions who pose as lumps of bent plastic. And nothing Jim Murphy can say or do will alter that impression in time to save his party.

Except for Viewers in Scotland

27 March 2015

What did we learn from the non-debate debate in which Ed Miliband and Davie Cameron didn't debate? The debate was really just an interrogation with Paxo who was clearly missing the monstering days of Newsnight when he got to dine on the fresh and quivering carcasses of politicians, it did not do much to add to the sum total of human enlightenment. Not that we'd have been any the wiser if the two of them had actually debated, we see them do that every week at Prime Minister's Questions in the House of Commons, and it typically consists of middle class schoolboys hurling none too witty insults at one another. Which doesn't even have much in the way of entertainment value, never mind edification.

So what did we actually learn from the night's proceedings? We learned that Davie Cameron is an out of touch toff who has not got the slightest idea how the rest of us live our lives. And we learned that Ed Miliband is an out of touch geek who has not got the slightest idea how the rest of us live our lives. It was like being invited to make a choice between a black and white episode of Upstairs Downstairs with no Downstairs, and a 1970s Open University broadcast on computer programming.

Most people would choose to switch off, at least anyone with a modicum of sanity.

Ed Miliband was asked whether he was tough enough to be Prime Minister, to which he gave a reply that was a doomed attempt to channel Dirty Harry. Admittedly the only magnum he's ever come anywhere near is the chocolate covered ice cream variety, but Ed's so tough he can bite into it straight out of the freezer. Hell yes, Ed's a tough and thick skinned geek, his fighting skills honed on the mean streets of Primrose Hill. He'll challenge people who don't pick up their dog's crap with really nasty looks, and he'll tsk furiously at littering, he'll protect the innocent in posh coffee bars from nasty spillages and bacon sandwiches with a ready supply of paper tissues. If you need someone to protect your back in a fight, you know that you can rely on Ed to organise a letter writing campaign to the Hampstead residents' monthly newsletter. Hell yes, bring it on. Ed's got mail merge at the ready. He can wield a Labour policy statement like Thor wields his hammer, how tough is that? Ed's as tough as guacamole and as threating as a flattened hedgehog. Ed's so tough that he's got street creds in two kitchens.

Yes, Labour got lots of things wrong, Ed admitted. They were wrong to allow the banks to regulate themselves. They were wrong about pretty much everything that happened over the course of the Blair and Brown years. But Ed wants us all to move on from that, which is politicospeak for let's pretend none of it ever happened and let's pretend that none of it will ever happen again. Even though it probably would, because this is the Labour party we're talking about here. But most of all, it means let's pretend that absolutely none of it is the fault of Eds Miliband or Balls.

When it was Davie's turn, he gave a very good impression of a man who really wished that he'd sent his butler to deal with all these troubling questions instead. The whole point of being a posh Tory is that one gets a little man in to do the heavy lifting. Or indeed the light lifting, or even any sort of lifting at all. Lifting? What's lifting? Isn't that a manual labour working class thing performed by oiks on a zero hours contract? Isn't that what an ATOS assessment is for?

When pressed, Davie admitted that he wouldn't like to live on the proceeds of a zero hours contract, even though such things are jolly good for the working class students who have to lift things to pay for their education. Davie didn't have to pay for his education himself, what with having a dad who was a millionaire.

Food banks? asked Davie, the only reason they're being used more is because - as an act of kindness - the Tories now allow them to be advertised in Job Centres. This also means that there are fewer people begging on the streets, since they can just go directly to the food bank and beg there. It's tidier all round. Following the success of this policy, Iain Duncan Smith is also now considering allowing Job Centres to advertise cliffs, bridges and high buildings which are ideal locations for depressed people who've been sanctioned to throw themselves off of. This will also reduce the unemployment statistics, making Tory economic policies seem like they're working. It's a win win, smiled Davie, all my rich pals think so.

Davie was forced to admit that he didn't actually know anyone personally who didn't have a personal fortune of less than ten million, or who earned less than his good friend Malkie Rifkind - who won't get out of bed for less than eight grand for a morning's work. Except his cleaner, he does know his cleaner, although he can't quite recall her name. Lovely woman, salt of the earth, and she does wonderful things with a can of Pledge. How do you think that Davie's face got so shiny?

By this time, faced with the utter bankruptcy of the UK's traditional two party system, the average voter will have switched off in disgust. This is it, this is what it's come to, our democratic choices reduced to picking between a useless geek who dreams he's Clint Eastwood, or an entitled Eton schoolboy who's had his entire life handed to him on a silver platter. Both of them offering slightly different flavoured servings of the same austerity pie - and you won't be getting a slice of anything anyway. Vote Humpty, or vote Dumpty, your prospects will still be falling off the wall.

You don't get any other choices UK voters - except, of course, for viewers in Scotland.

102,143 and Counting

28 March 2015

This weekend is the party conference of a party that's not a branch office or an accounting unit. And it's actually being attended by real live human beings who are filling a large hall. Over 3000 folk have turned up to listen to politics on a Saturday morning in Glasgow in March, representatives of a truly Scottish party that now has 102,143 members and counting. Account for that, accounting unit. It's a nation in motion and it's not going to stop until it achieves the change we've demanded, the change that's been promised. The change that Westminster said it would deliver but it reneged on. We're going to take it from them.

Labour won't give an account of how many members its accounting unit has, and the reason they won't give an exact figure is because the number is embarrassingly low. 7,000 if they're lucky, and counting down. Tick tock. And another one leaves. 6,999 / 102,144.

It's a number that is getting smaller every day as Labour's dwindling band of non-elected activists give up in despair. Tick tock. It's going to be 6,998 by the time I get to the end of this sentence. They have so few left that they can't deliver their election propaganda and have to get the post office to do it. Tick tock. 6,997 / 102,145.

274

Compare and contrast the buzz in the packed hall with anything that the accounting units can manage. Labour's carefully stage managed speeches before small gatherings of pre-selected safe types who won't ask difficult questions. The tumbleweed in the Lib Dem room. The Tories who can't count past one. Yet Scotland is engaged with politics, engaged with discussion and debate about its future. Politicians bewail and bemoan the public disenchantment with politics. Well here were are in Scotland enchanted with the possibilities this country has. We're exciting and exciting, we're alive to ideas, we're more pregnant than a panda. But the Unionist politicians are scared and angry, because we're not engaged with anything that the Smugurph has to offer. But then Jim is deeply unengaging. Would you want to be trapped in a lift with him? Nuff said. Tick tock, 6,996 / 102,146.

In a doomed effort to wrest some headlines from the force that really will shape Scotland's general election, Gordie Broon today promised that this election would be the "social justice" election and promised all sorts of goodies for NHS Scotland. Gordie's going to guarantee that, just like he guaranteed his precious vow, and just like he guaranteed to be the MP for Kirkcaldy. He'll guarantee it by pissing off and delivering well paid speeches to rich business people. He'll guarantee it by getting confused between powers that are devolved and those that are retained by Westminster. But that's Gordie, confused and lost in a political wasteland of his own making. He still believes he's the king over the water, the rest of us know that he drowned a long time ago. Tick tock, 6,995 / 102,147.

But today is Nicola's day. She's the good cop to Alicsammin's bad cop, trapping the Westminster parties in a pincer movement, and grabbing them by the bollocks that they constantly spout. Alicsammin spent the week putting the shiters up them, now Nicola comes with the soothing balm that will dissolve the nasty haemorrhoids of Tory rule. She's promising to be the constructive force for progressive politics that Labour once said it would be, but instead Labour turned into a bonfire of hope courtesy of Gordie and Tony Blair. Tick tock, 6,994 / 102,148.

Nicola showed why Labour hates the SNP so much, because she is promising the kind of policies that Labour used to promise when it was still a labour party when it really was the party of the workers' expectations and hadn't become what it is today, the party of managing the workers' expectations. The difference is that Nicola means what she says. She means it when she says she wants a living wage, no privatisation in the NHS, no student fees, an end to Trident, abolishing the House of Lords, proportional representation, gender equality. And home rule, the promise made by Keir Hardie all those generations ago. We've been promised these things for decades, but Labour's no closer to delivering them. The British Parliamentary Road to socialism ended in a PPI contract and a toll booth. It's time to take matters out of Labour's hands. It's time to hold the accounting unit to account. Tick tock. 6,993 / 102,149.

The question Labour needs to answer is if the combined number of Labour and SNP MPs can attain a majority in Westminster then will Labour rule out letting Cameron back into power. Jim Murphy doesn't want an answer to that question. Jim Murphy doesn't want his accounting unit to be held to account. He doesn't want to be forced to be the socialist he discovered that he must claim to be ever since he found out that being a Blairite was electoral poison. Nicola's going to force him. Tick tock. 6,992 / 102,150.

So here we are. Standing at the gates of history. Standing at the door of change, pushing through. Nothing stands between us and destiny except Jim and his discredited lies, the tissue of mendacity that is all that holds back the Scottish tide. We only have to have the courage to walk through the portcullis of Westminster and Scotland will change the world. And we have that in abundance. Scotland has already changed forever, already crossed into the land of self-belief. We're independent in our heads already, we're independent in our hearts, we're independent in our spirit - and that's all we need. Tick tock. 6,991 / 102,151.

It's too late to stop us. We're already here. We are in your town, your street, your house. The numbers are counting the future, and the future is Scottish, the future is here. You are the future. Be it.

Tick tock.

The Definition of Fairness

30 March 2015

So that's it then, the Coalition formally ended last night at midnight as the Westminster Parliament dissolved itself in a vat of acid. OK, not that last bit, a spot of wishful thinking there. The really good news, people of the East End of Glasgow, is that Magrit Curran isn't our MP now. And it's looking as though she never will be again. That's got to be worth a wee rejoice or three, or four.

Magrit was in the papers today, trying to save her job. She wants us to know that if we don't vote for her and her pals, Scotland will no longer become the most fair country in the history of fairness. That's Labour fairness, the fairness that introduced zero hours contracts, PPI rip offs, presided over growing inequality, let the banks run riot, did nothing to tackle the gross imbalance in Scottish land ownership and allowed one of the most resource rich countries in Europe to allegedly become a financial basket case dependent upon hand-outs from Westminster. The fairness that took what was once a left wing party and moved it further to the right than the pre-Thatcherite Tories. The Labour party whose sole selling point is that it is not the Conservative party that it increasingly resembles. That Labour fairness. And to think if we vote SNP we might put all that at risk and drag

Labour kicking and screaming back to the centre ground. No wonder Magrit is appalled.

But then Magrit has become a by-word for counter factual statements which are dressed up in Labour press releases and published in the papers and broadcast on the telly. And are then, gobsmackingly, taken seriously by serious people who you'd think really ought to know better. Scotland is a country whose media lets it be patronised by Magrit Curran. That's Labour fairness. Vote Labour and be patronised by self-serving morons.

Not that Magrit can really be blamed, and not only because nothing is ever Magrit or the Labour party's fault. She can't be blamed because she's only acting like Labour MPs have always acted. Besides, if you look up the word magritcurran in a Scots dictionary it's defined as "to be in a state of self-aggrandising delusion, hallucinatory". As in: "I'm sorry I can't do anything productive at work today, I've come over a bit magritcurran. But I'll still be claiming my expenses."

It's not just Magrit whose relationship to reality is tangential at best. Jim Murphy seems to have forgotten that he's a Labour MP, at least if his election leaflets are anything to go by. In a shameless attempt to appeal to the Tory voters of East Renfrew, Jim's election leaflets don't once mention that he's a Labour MP. It's a terribly Tory tactic. David Mundell's election leaflets likewise fail to mention he's Scotland's only Conservative MP.

It's not like we were voting Labour for any positive reasons. Labour stopped having anything positive to offer a generation ago. In some ways, the Unionist parties are misnamed by those of us who support independence. They're not so much supporters of the Union as opposed to anything which might reduce their own power and influence. Desperateselfishbastertists would be a better term for the Labour-Tory-Lib Dem axis.

Labour MPs in Scotland behave like they do because they've been able to get away with it. They've been effectively unaccountable representatives of an unaccountable accounting unit. And we must take responsibility for allowing them to get away with it by blindly voting for them in such large numbers that they were able to take us for granted, simply in order to keep out something that was worse. But it didn't work. Voting Labour doesn't keep the Tories out. It's their sole selling point, and it's not even true. Voting Labour is like buying a toothpaste made entirely out of sugar in the hope it will protect you from tooth decay.

We've begged them to change. We've pleaded. We've sent sharply worded letters of complaint to the editor of the Herald. We voted them out at Holyrood. Nothing worked. Scotland's Labour MPs remain as entitled as lairds with their vast fiefdoms. So it's time for a peasants' revolt. It's the only way to put an end to being patronised by the self-serving morons in the pages of the press and in the TV studios.

Scotland, despite us being constantly told by the desperateselfishbastertists that we're the most devolviest and fairest country that's not really a country in the history of happy unions of nations, doesn't have a representative media. Uniquely amongst self-governing nations we don't have control over our own broadcasting. This leads to the surreal situation where the Westminster Parliament and MPs for Sussex had to be consulted when there were proposals for a Gaelic language telly channel. Apparently the issue of whether Postman Pat should be broadcast in Gaelic is on immense concern in the pubs of Lewes as well as Lewis. It also leads to Scottish viewers hearing more on the news about the educational and health systems in England than about those in Scotland. It means we have to keep hearing about bloody UKIP, a party which only got the meagre support it has in Scotland because it's never off the bloody BBC. It means Nigel Farage is always on the telly with that smug look like a teenager who's just discovered masturbation. But then Nigel doesn't really need to masturbate because he's got the BBC to stroke him instead.

It means Scotland has no national forum in which to discuss national concerns. This is Magrit's fairness. Scotland's distinctiveness is subsumed into the larger UK and prevented from being too different in case it gives us ideas above our proper station in life, which is to act as a spot of Caledonian ethnic colour in the patchwork of Britishness, allowing the desperateselfishbastertist parties to pretend that British nationalism isn't really nationalism at all.

A Scottish national public broadcaster might not let the Labour accounting unit get away with shamelessly conflating devolved issues with those reserved to Westminster. It might ask the Labour party why it's banging on about the NHS in a Westminster election when the NHS is controlled by Holyrood not Westminster. It might ask Jim Murphy why he's so ashamed and embarrassed by the very party he purports to lead that he can't even bring himself to mention it on his own election leaflets. Those would be fair questions. We can vote Labour, and get Magrit's definition of fairness, or we can vote to define fairness for ourselves.

Waving from the Quayside

31 March 2015

Polly Toynbee, doyen of the Islington Labouristas and one time cheerleader for Tony Blair and Gordie Broon, has ventured north of the M25 and come to visit Scotland - and it's not even the Embra Festival. There's true dedication to the cause of writing apologias for you, or is that apologii. Anyway, in the opinion of Polly, Scotland's about to drift off from the Union, sailing off into a state of independence almost by accident. She takes two conclusions from this, firstly that Scotland drifting off into independence is a very bad thing, and therefore following on from this as a natural logical consequence, it must all be the fault of the Tories. And there was you and me thinking that it was all Alicsammin's fault, because everything else usually is.

Polly complains that David Cameron has never governed for a united kingdom, but instead has implemented policies which benefit his core voters in the leafier parts of the south. And this is perfectly true, although it's an observation which is unlikely to make anyone slap their foreheads and go "Oh. My. God. I never realised." Being selfish evil basterts is pretty much the definition of Tory, so it's not like this is news. Just look at Iain Duncan Smith, if you can bear it, which few can. But being selfish evil basterts is written into the DNA of

283

Torydom, and it is a fact that the word Tory comes from the Gaelic word *tòraigh*, which can be loosely translated as 'selfish evil thieving bastert'. It's a less well known fact that the word toerag is from the Gaelic diminutive of *tòraigh*, and when you call someone a toerag you are in fact calling them a dwarfish Osborne, and that could mentally scar a small child for life. And for once I'm not actually making this up. At least not much.

Of course, Polly's definition of "very bad thing" is absolutely anything which doesn't benefit the Westminster Labour party. Polly wants Scotland to vote for a party that abandoned it a generation ago to keep out a party that abandoned it two generations ago.

However, in her rush to blame the Tories for everything, which to be fair isn't unreasonable, Polly ignores the fact that Labour has never governed for a united kingdom either, treating Scotland, the North of England, and Wales as fiefdoms whose sole purpose is to provide lobby fodder so Labour too can appeal to those better off voters in the leafier parts of the south. It's what kept Tony Blair in power for over a decade. So maybe it's just not outside the bounds of possibility that the setting sail of the Scottish independence ship is the fault of all the miserable short sighted triangulating lot of them together. Who's Better Together now eh.

In Islington Labour commentariat world, Scottish independence is a bad thing because it no longer means a block of 40 odd lobby fodder MPs blindly doing whatever it is that the Labour whips tell them to do. Unlike Islington apologists for the Labour party, yer actual traditional Labour supporters in places like Shettleston and Sheffield have long since worked out that blindly supporting the Labour party by providing placepersons with the personality of placemats to blindly do what the whips say does not do a great deal to improve their lives and circumstances. Labour has given us generations of neglect, generations of apathy, generations of hopelessness. The only thing Labour has positively generated in the East End of Glasgow is the impressive expenses claims of Magrit Curran, following in the impressive tradition of the unlamented David Marshall. He's kept very quiet over the past few years hasn't he.

The sense of despair and anger is the same in Shettleston and Sheffield, the difference is that voters in Shettleston have something they can do about it. In the case of Shettleston, that something comes in the shape of the SNP. And that's why those of us who, unlike Magrit, actually live in the East End are telling everyone we can to get angry, get even, and vote SNP.

Similar advice applies in other parts of Scotland. If you don't live in the East End of Glasgow you can vote for the lovely Anne McLaughlin in Glasgow North East, or Emma Harper, the nurse in the Borders who wants to make the Tories extinct.

Scotland getting even is the real motor of this election campaign. We're out for revenge, and it's a dish best served in the gloomy faces of Labour commentators on the telly on election night as they desperately try to tell us why losing almost all their seats isn't that bad really. I want to see Magrit Curran as a runner up. I want to see Jim Murphy as the unelectable leader of a fictional party that doesn't exist.

Labour can promise whatever it likes, £1 billion last week, £800 million this week, beads and blankets, free pixies and stardust sandwiches for every pensioner, but no one believes them anymore. They've lied so much in the past that they have no credibility left. They deserted Scotland but demand our votes simply because they're not the Tories. That worked as long as it was a binary choice, as long as there was a switch with only two settings. The switch got broken in the referendum campaign, and it was Labour that broke it. Now we're going to get even. This is the long slow run up, the pulling of the foot, the taking aim. Labour's going to get kicked in the nads. The only question left is how high up their lying throats their nads are going to get kicked.

What we learned during the referendum campaign is that Scotland will not be passive, we will not be silent. We will be the agents of our own change. We are the wind in our own sails and this ship is sailing and we're setting the course. Labour is left floundering in deep and stormy water of its own creation.

Polly can wave from the quayside as she watches her party drown.

By the Power of Numbskull

1 April 2015

Poor Jim Murphy, he's getting increasingly desperate as he runs on empty to destination nowhere, and still no one likes him. Even most of his own party can't abide him - especially not most of his own party, as those poor benighted basterts actually have to deal with him face to face. Poor poor Jim, naebdie is sticking their paycard in the Labourometer, the lights are going out, and his gas is going peep. Poor Jim, everyone hates him and no one cares.

Jim spent much of Wednesday making increasingly hysterical claims. The SNP are Cameron's litle helpers, they're in league with Satan, they're the minor demons in the service of Be'elzecameron. The SNP sacrifices Curran chickens on the altar of Osborne. Jim stands alone as the guardian of the gates of Hades, keeping out the saltire face painted hell hordes armed with nothing more than an irn bru crate and the BBC Scotland news department on speed dial.

How can the SNP possibly target hard working honest Labour MPs who've never pauchled their expenses that much. It's wrong. It's unfair. And by trying to unseat Labour MPs the SNP is doing the Tories' work for them. Because it's only the Tories who are allowed to target

Labour MPs. The SNP have no business getting involved in a British election. Didn't Jim win the referendum for the Union armed with nothing more than an egg stained shirt and a megaphone so that Scotland could keep on having British elections? And where's the thanks he gets eh? Bunch of ingrates, thae voters. Voters in Scotland are not supposed to think, they're not supposed to make decisions. That sort of thing ought to be left to the likes of Jim.

Only the Tories have proprietary rights to attack Labour in Scotland in Jim's mental universe. Which is just as well for Jim, because the Tories in Scotland have an even worse aim than the baddies in a Bruce Willis movie, and would never be able to take a pot shot at Jim as he jogs along in Eastwood. Jim's a superhero, in his own mind if nowhere else, and he's going to save the Labour party in Scotland so he's got a career and can get on the telly.

Jim's a superhero with a special superhero costume and a special superhero superpower. His supercostume is a Scotland top and his superpower is amnesia. He'll fly into action from the giddy heights of an irn bru crate. He'll yell at the media with the power of a megaphone. Jim's forgotten that he's not a socialist, he's forgotten that he actively campaigned and bullied in order to get student fees introduced. He's forgotten all about the Iraq war, privatisation, Tony Blair and sooking up to bankers. He hopes that the rest of us have forgotten too. By the power of numbskull!

Poor Jim Murphy. There he is a superhero with superpowers and the only power he's got is the power to make Labour MPs vanish. Watch Magrit Curran fade away! See Jimmy Hood disappear! Anas Sarwar will inherit no more, Tom Harris will sink without a trace. Jim has achieved great things, and he's done it all just by being himself and not the person he wants us to think he is. That's Jim's other superpower, but not the one he wants - we can see right through him.

In years to come this will be Jim's legacy. He'll be the fag end of the Labour party in Scotland. He's the footnote, the epitaph, the full stop. Jim's the little bit of concentrated poison at the end of a long drag that produces the death rattle. And in the history books it will be Jim's name that's mentioned when academics discuss how the Labour party died in Scotland, forever associated with killing the party he swore he'd save. Labour in Scotland was born in hope, conceived in fine ideals. It died with Jim's spinning frantically with notes on his sleeve scribbled by John McTernan, trying shift Scotland further to the right than Ted Heath, trying to get Ed Miliband elected. Labour in Scotland died, not with a bang, but with a wimp.

Poor Jim, all those lies, all those untruths, all those half-truths, all those stains on his soul, and all for Naughtie on Radio 4. Jim's upset at the arrogance of the SNP, how dare they think they might win. That's supposed to him that's being arrogant, he's had a lifetime's practice for this moment. He was the big hitter, the superhero superstar, feted by the press, hailed by the media. He had his moment in the sun in the winter in Scotland. It didn't go to plan. Poor Jim.

Jim was going to give the little people what for, he was going to put them in their place. Jim was going to smash the Alicsamminites and smite the Sturgeonistas. Jim had superpowers and a picture in the Guardian with a halo around his head. He was going to walk on the troubled water of the referendum, he was going to turn Labour's rancid fish and wee bit of stale bread into a feast and feed the feeble forty. Jim was going to bring the lost Scottish sheep home, with his superpower of amnesia and his quiet voice and his McTernan dog whistles. It's going to take a lot more than a miracle to save Labour's sorry arses.

But the lost Scottish sheep have other ideas. We're not fooled by Jim trying to herd us and take our dreams to the abattoir. Because it's not us who're in for the chop Jim, that would be you. Labour's headed for the knacker's yard, and there's no superpower on earth that's going to stop it.

Poor Jim Murphy. It's almost possible to feel sorry for him as he stares oblivion and humiliation and disgrace in the face. Almost, but then you look at Jim as he spins and he lies and dissembles, and you think to yourself - couldn't happen to a more deserving man.

Here Come the Girls

2 April 2015

L et's have a heated debate! The party leaders lined up on Thursday evening to take turns at bashing David Cameron, because, let's face it, he deserves it. It looked a bit like an afternoon gameshow, which to be honest isn't far off the mark. It's just seven to one instead of fifteen to one.

Quite shockingly, when reading the leaders' biographies before the gameshow - sorry, the debate - I discovered that I am older than all seven of the party leaders and I'm not even that close to claiming my alicsammin buspass. But I'm even older than Nigel, which is gobsmacking, since I had always thought that Nigel Farage had been brought to us from the 1950s.

The three female leaders were there too, invited only because the broadcasters ran out of excuses not to invite any women after insisting that Nigel Farage had to be there because they reckon he gives good TV. It's that post-masturbation smug grin of his, amazingly there are people in this world who are not put off by it.

For the Greens Natalie Bennett started by telling us that there's no need for austerity. She was followed by Nigel, the gameshow had only just started and already Nige was putting all the blame on immigrants. Nick Clegg said he was really really sorry for everything. Nicola promised the hand of friendship to people across the rest of the UK and told them that together, hand in hand, we can give Westminster an almighty kick in the nads and get rid of Trident and austerity at the same time, which got a cheer from me.

Davie did his middle class patronising thing, like he was a Scottish political commentator complaining about working class people not being respectful enough when they talk about politics, and this time Dave wasn't agreeing with Nick. They were followed by Lianne Wood who broke the world record for the number of times that anyone has ever said Plaid Cymru on telly. Then Ed Miliband got his forefingers and thumb stuck together with superglue and told us he wanted to be prime minister.

Ed kept looking directly at the camera and waving his superglued hand at us. Nigel Farage had a very shiny face and kept interjecting excitedly like a chimpanzee that had just discovered a barrel load of amphetamines. Nigel told us he was pissed off that "the canny Scots" were getting lots of freebies courtesy of the English taxpayer and said that Scotland should get less money. Nicola told him he was talking out of his monkey bum and pointed out that Scotland paid more in taxes. Then she laid into Ed Miliband, who was doing his best to keep his head down while he separated his forefingers from his thumb, for supporting the Tories' austerity plans.

Where are the 12 billion cuts in benefits coming from? Which benefits are going to be cut? Nicola demanded that Davie spell that out. Who is going to lose out? Davie didn't answer. Then Nigel got his chance and he blamed it all on foreigners again.

Why does Ed keep staring unblinkingly at the camera when he's answering a point put to him by someone standing right beside him? It's starting to creep me out.

The second question was about the NHS and how we can ensure that it's properly funded. Nige got to answer first and he blamed it all on foreigners again, if the UK didn't have to give money away to foreigners it could afford to abolish car parking charges at hospitals. Nicola pointed out that car parking charges at hospitals have already been abolished in Scotland and said that the SNP was utterly opposed to the creeping privatisation introduced by Labour and pursued with gusto by the Tories and the Lib Dems. All over England and Wales people were watching her and going "Ooooh so that's why they wanted independence."

Then there was some more waffle from the main Westminster party leaders and Ed Miliband did his unblinking staring at the cameras thing again. His fingers are still superglued together. This might be because in previous telly debates he's done the waggy finger thing, but it was pointed out that this is a gesture most often found in the videos of suicide bombers and isn't a good look for someone who wants to be prime minister. So the Labour PR folk got out the superglue. It's as plausible as any other explanation.

Don't ask me what any of them were saying, because by this point I was thinking that we're less than halfway through the proceedings and I was wondering whether I could cheer myself up by self-harming. Then Nigel blamed the problems of the NHS on foreigners with HIV and instead of self-harm I nearly harmed the TV screen with a shoe.

Davie's speaking now. I can summarise it for you: "Lie lie lie lie lie, irrelevant, dissembling, lie, shiny face, smug git, lie." Not coincidentally this is also the content of every Tory party political broadcast for the past 100 years.

Dear God, and it's only half time. It's at times like this I wonder why I ever gave up drugs. It's immigration next apparently. Nigel's gone on about little else for the past hour.

A wifie asks how the parties would deal with immigration. Ed does a staring eyed sub-Nigel impression. I'm really getting freaked out when Ed stares at the camera with his superglued fingers. He doesn't blink. Are his eyelids superglued too? He looks like he's wondering whether he's left the gas on in one of his kitchens. This is the burning question of Ed's election campaign so far.

Lianne Wood speaks some sense. The problems of this country were not caused by Polish building site workers but by bankers and the financial industry - by people like Nigel Farage come to think of it. Then Nicola gets to weigh in with actual facts and stuff and shows that it's the women in this debate who are the only ones acting like grown-ups. Ed's still staring unblinkingly directly at the camera. I am seriously freaked out and don't think I'll sleep tonight. Davie came out with more shiny lies. But it's Nigel who is really excited and happy now, the pub bore who's allowed to bore on national TV on his favourite boreathon.

Davie said that there are three sides to the coin on immigration. Eh? Not entirely sure what shape his money is, and you'd think he'd know what with having a personal fortune in the millions.

Nicola said that it's important to remember that diversity is a strength. See what I mean about women talking sense? She's actually making a plea for a sensible and fact based discussion about immigration in a room with Nigel Farage in it. Ye're on a hiding to nothing there Nicola, but kudos for trying. The women are streets ahead in this debate.

Ed's staring unblinkingly at the camera again. His fingers are still stuck together. I'm scared. He keeps talking about those of us at home. At home, like he's going to come and glue our fingers together. Davie Cameron weighs in, having lost his three sided coin, there's no point trying to give a precis of what he's saying because now all the men are shouting at once and in any case if it comes out of Davie's mooth it's bound to be a lie.

Nicola tries to get Davie, Ed and Nick to agree that since they were telling us last year that we're a happy family of nations that none of the nations of the UK will be dragged out of the EU against its will. None of them answer.

Last question now. Thank god. A student sitting in front of a man with a seriously impressive moustache asks what the leaders will do for young people, who are faced with being worse off than their parents. Cue some meaningless waffle from Ed and Davie. Davie answers her by going on about pensions, because pensioners are young people as far as Tories are concerned. Nick Clegg comes across surprisingly well, although no one is going to forget that he's still a lying bastert - he begs forgiveness for the student fees thing, but he's not going to get any. The cameras cut back to the questioner and the background moustache. Neither look that impressed.

Nicola points out that in Scotland we don't have tuition fees. She tells us that she's from a working class family and is only standing there now because she got a free education. It's morally wrong of politicians to deprive young people of the same chances that they themselves got. She gets a round of applause from the audience. Then it's Nigel, who blames it all on abolishing grammar schools, and foreigners, or possibly foreigners who abolished grammar schools.

Then there's some general shouting between the men as they all blame one another for the financial crisis - the fact that they're all equally to blame doesn't seem to occur to them. Natalie Bennett gets to speak and reminds them that they're supposed to be talking about education.

Ooooh we've got a heckler. A woman stands up during a Camerondrone and says that the boys aren't listening and aren't addressing the concerns of the questioners.

296

Cameron says that we have brilliant armed forces, let's say thanks. Smug patronising git. The woman in the audience yells: "Shut up! We have veterans homeless on our streets!"

Gaun yersel hen! At last, a real human gets to speak unscripted. There's an off camera slamming of a door. She got ejected. Proles shouldn't make sensible points without permission.

The only people saying anything sensible in this debate are women. The parties which are opposed to austerity and the old boys' network are represented by women. The parties which seek to change the system to make it fairer and more representative are led by women. Can you spot a wee theme here? It's clear now - in Scotland vote SNP, in Wales vote Plaid, and in England vote Green. Here come the girls.

Plus Ça Change, Plus C'est la Même Chose

4 April 2015

A wee while ago there was a meeting between La Nicla, which is defined in French dictionaries as "*la femme qui puts les shiteurs up l'establaissment britannique*", and the French ambassador. The purpose of the meeting may or may not have been to have a wee laugh at George Osborne's attempts to make political capital out of the Battle of Agincourt, but La Nicla and L'Ambassadeuse had a wee natter over some Ferrero Rocher about things that diplomatic protocol says that ambassadors and first ministers should have a wee natter about, and as is normal minutes were taken and a report was sent as a matter of courtesy to the UK Foreign Office.

There is apparently no truth in the rumour that the minutes of the meeting were taken by someone on work placement from Reporting Scotland, but since the British media doesn't feel the need to check their sources, why the hell should I?

Then yesterday amidst great fanfare, a story was published in the Telegraph, a paper which prefers to overlook stories which are negative for large banks with advertising accounts in the Telegraph, claiming that the paper had received a leak of a Foreign Office memo which said that La Nicla wanted Davie Cameron to be the next Prime Minister and had said that Ed Miliband wasn't fit for the job. This is of course directly contrary to the SNP's entire electoral strategy, and if true would be devastating. The problem for the Telegraph is that it isn't true. But the Telegraph was too busy rounding up the usual suspects to stick the boot into the SNP to bother checking the facts.

The paper managed to get quotes on how shocking this was from an outrage of Labour politicians - that's the proper collective noun in case you were wondering - Labour politicos were disgusted that a party was saying one thing in public and another in private. How dare the SNP act like the Labour party, being duplicitous is Jim Murphy's job. The Telegraph even managed to get a quote from Wullie Rennie, who was probably just pleased that anyone other than regular passengers on the number 17 bus to Kelty had noticed that he exists.

But after taking the time to ask the usual hating the SNP suspects to give quotes about how appalled they were, what Simon No-Honestly-I'm-a-Proper-Reporter Johnson failed to do was to ask anyone who was actually present at the meeting to comment on the contents of a memo which gave a fourth hand account of what was supposedly said at a meeting that the memo writer did not attend. You know, the kind of thing that budding reporters get taught in their very first class in journalism school, the class entitled "Checking sources : How to do your fucking job".

The source in question, La Nicla, immediately denied there was any truth in the tale. The Labour party tutted, "Well she would say that wouldn't she?" Now La Nicla may be many things, but she's hardly likely to undermine the SNP's entire election strategy in a meeting which is minuted, even if it were true that she wants Cameron to win the election in England, which she doesn't.

Then the French weighed in, and denied the story with a firm, "*Non, absolutemente non.*" Labour said, well they would say that, what with being foreign and probably immigrants. I made that up of course, but sauce for the goose and all that. I could make up another quote from Jim Murphy at this juncture, but he was doing that quiet voice thing that he always does when he's trying to make out that he's a serious statesperson and I couldn't hear him over Kezia Dugdale's screams.

Everyone who was at the meeting or anywhere in the vicinity denied the Telegraph story even before the sole copy of the paper sold in Glasgow hit the newsstand. The only person who hasn't denied anything, or been quoted on anything - apart from La Nicla and the French ambassador - is the Scottish Secretary of State, Alistair Koalamichael. He was the other person who met with the French ambassador that day. Alistair has been keeping his head down and has been very quiet indeed. He's hoping no one will ask him where the memo came from.

The icing on the brioche and the need for the Telegraph's ace reporter to, you know, do his fucking job, was illustrated by the final sentence in the very same memo that the Telegraph published in defence of a story that was deflating more quickly than Jim Murphy's reputation as saviour of the Labour party in Scotland. The final sentence read: "I have to admit that I'm not sure that the FM's tongue would be quite so loose on that kind of thing in a meeting like that, so it might well be a case of something being lost in translation."

So even the un-named person who drafted the memo was uncertain about the truth of the allegation. But none of this stopped the Telegraph rushing into print with it without doing the most cursory of checks.

Despite the story being shot down in flames even before the Telegraph had a chance to be ripped up and used to light a coal fire, this didn't stop Ed Miliband appearing on the telly to denounce the SNP on the back of a discredited tale. He's still waving those superglued fingers. This all by itself proves that Ed isn't fit to be Prime Minister, his willingness to associate himself with a baseless smear that is - although the superglued fingers don't help -but then Ed learned his politics in the office of Gordie Broon, the man who saw fit to employ Damien the Omen McBride.

An official inquiry into the "leak" has been announced. It will doubtless be a whitewash. But there are serious questions to be answered here - not the least of which is who in the Foreign Office was prepared to do serious damage to the UK's diplomatic relationship with France in order to score cheap party political points in an election. And there was us thinking that the civil service was supposed to be neutral.

But here's the real lesson to learn from this debacle. Labour had a whole load of attacks ready to launch on social media within minutes of the Telegraph breaking the story on Friday night. So clearly Labour had been well briefed in advance that the story was going to be published. Instead of it being a story about how the SNP secretly favours the Tories, it's now a story about how Labour is - yet again - cosying up to and colluding with the Tory establishment just like they did during the referendum campaign. Labour and the Tories, twin cheeks du même cul. *Plus ça change, plus c'est la même chose.*

Jim Murphy BA Politics (Failed)

6 April 2015

The fallout from the Nickileaks saga is still falling on the benighted heids of the Unionist parties. The forces of the British Establishment ganged up to keep the Most Dangerous Woman in Britain at bay, only they didn't do it very well, which is only to be expected when your lead conspirator is Alistair Carmichael, a man who can't even conspire to take a leak without it dribbling all down his leg. These things happen, don't they Alistair. Well we don't know for certain it was Alistair who was responsible for the leakage, but then I'm adopting Daily Telegraph standards of journalistic integrity. So that makes it all just fine, and we can expect Ed Miliband to take everything in this blog as gospel truth.

The Most Dangerous Woman in Britain has turned their attacks against them. She's battering them on the head with rolled up copy of the Telegraph, slapping them on their lardy arses with a papier-mâché bat made from Daily Mail slur stories, and treading them into dust with those tartan high heels of hers. She's laid down a challenge to the wide open eyes of Ed Miliband to join with her in opposing the Tories - and now we know he's staring like that because he's looking directly into the headlights of an oncoming Caledonian Express. The happy warrior is not a happy Easter bunny.

Meanwhile Alistair himself has, according to the Daily Record, "fingered the civil servant responsible" for creating the big stain down the front of the Koalamichael's troosers, and there was you thinking that sexual harrassment was illegal in modern Scotland. However, Alistair's not for saying who the person is, and far less is he going to take any action against them. Which means that either Alistair is a terribly understanding and indulgent employer, or the leaker had good reason to believe that Alistair was giving them the nod on the quiet. We'll have to wait for the inquiry to find out which is the case, but not to worry, British government enquiries always clear things up to everyone's satisfaction, don't they.

Conveniently the enquiry won't report back until after the election and after everyone involved is brain dead, which in Alistair's case happened quite some time ago. But for those of us who aren't brain dead, that only leaves us with truthiness. Which of those two scenarios seems more plausible to you? Are Alistair's pants on fire, or is he just looking a bit sweaty? Alistair Koalamichael is doing his very best to keep out of the limelight, and that's not hard for a man who is so far up himself that it takes a colonoscopy to find him. My money is on the inflammable underwear.

It's odd that the actual Tories in Scotland, those few that remain, were not contacted by the Torygraph so they could be outraged by the news that Nicola supposedly wants them to remain in power. The paper contacted Labour and Wullie Rennie. Because when there's an important national story breaking which looks like it might have an immediate and decisive impact on a national election, Wullie Rennie is the first person you turn to. At least it is if you're Alistair Carmichael.

The Labour party was fully involved in the production of this wee wheeze and thought they could get Nicola bang to rights - look she's to rights like the Tories, they screamed in orchestrated unison, in time to the beat of the Tory press. Oooooh, pursed lipped Smugurphy said, aren't the SNP the Tories' little helpers just like I said in that press release John McTernan wrote for me just a few days ago. But the story fell apart even before any ink had smeared itself on the Telegraph's printing press and Jim was covered in it looking like the opportunistic clown that we all know he really is.

Then Ed Miliband, with that masterful sense of timing and nose for the political zeitgeist which typifies the modern Labour party, managed to leap onto a bandwagon which had already careened off a cliff. Way to go to look statesmanlike and prime ministerial Ed. And it's entirely his own fault for listening to the Smugurph. Come the next election, it's going to be Scotland that superglues Ed's wavy fingers and sticks it to him.

The BBC and the rest of the discredited media are still trotting out the allegations in the memo, even though the allegations have been killed, cremated, and their ashes scattered on the grave of the Labour party in Scotland. They know that it's untrue, they know it's a lie, but are determined to keep playing what if, in the vain hope that there might be someone somewhere in Scotland who is going to have their mind changed. But our minds are already made up, and we've decided that we're pissed off at being patronised by idiots.

These are, let us remember, the same people who are always telling us that there needs to be more respect and decorum in politics. Politics are dragged into disrepute by working class people using working class language to slag off duplicitous lying basterts, they tell us while they play their infantile games. We must be respectful and stop saying childish things like Morphy Jim or the Smugurph and call Mr Murphy by his proper name and full title - so that would be: Jim Murphy BA Politics (failed).

And he's fully living up to the name, having failed quite spectacularly this time. It hasn't even taken him nine years. He's only been the leader of the Labour party Scottish accounting unit for a few short months. That's as close as Jim Murphy BA Politics (failed) is ever going to get to providing value for money. Jim and Labour in Scotland are, in the words of a Labour MP quoted in today's Herald, at defcon fucked.

Today Jim Murphy BA Politics (failed) is in the Guardian, reduced to begging Scotland not to vote SNP out of anger at Labour. We are angry Jim, we're angry with you, and we're voting to get rid of you because your politics are the politics of abasement, the politics of the gutter, the politics of despair, the politics of cynical lies. We're going to vote for the Scottish branch of the Occupy

Westminster Movement, and we will make the changes that Jim will never implement himself.

We're voting Jim, for a future that doesn't have you and your style of cynical politics in it.

A Cold Quiet Place of Clarity

7 April 2015

Jim Murphy BA Politics (failed) wants us not to vote against Labour in anger. I'd just like to take a few minutes out of a busy day spent beelin' to assure Jim that there are very few voters left in Scotland who will vote against the party in anger. Anger is not a strong enough word for what yer average Scottish voter feels for the Labour party in Scotland and what it has become. Anger doesn't begin to describe it.

Speaking for myself, I left anger behind a long time ago when Blair invaded Iraq and Jim cheered along. I took a wee detour by contempt when Labour let the bankers off their leash and Jim urged them on. I spent some time in apoplexy when Labour introduced the creeping back door privatisation of PPI contracts and Jim gave it his support. I had a holiday in derision when Gordie saved the world and Jim claimed some reflected glory. I made a stop-over in invective when Jim stood on an Irn Bru crate shoulder to shoulder with the Tories during the referendum campaign. And now Jim, now, I'm in that cold quiet place of clarity that tells me your party must be culled and your career killed off. I'm way past angry.

Labour only knows smear and fear, the disgrace is all theirs. The smears don't work anymore and all that the likes of Wee Dougie Alexander can do is to delete the evidence of his complicity in smear and hope that no one remembers. But we do remember Dougie. And we'll still remember in a few short weeks' time when we get to give you a verdict. It will be a sentence that's hard for Labour.

They can't say we didn't warn them. We warned them in 2007 and they promised they'd listen and change. They did neither. We gave them an almighty kicking in 2011 and they promised they'd listen and they'd change. They did neither. We put them on probation with the result of the independence referendum, and they went back to their old duplicity and lies. Their condition is terminal, and it's time to terminate them.

When the Labour party in Scotland chose Jim as its leader, it was the sad and sorry fag end of a party which had sucked all the life out of itself and the communities it claimed to represent. Jim's leadership is the cold dout in Labour's ashtray, the stale smell of Labour's decay and death, a party that's incapable of even recognising what its core voters long for and aspire to, never mind representing them. If anything resembling Labour's socialism, or even social democracy, is to be reborn then it can only come out of the scattered ashes of a party that traduced the hopes and aspirations of an entire people over three generations. Labour in Scotland must be killed off so something new can be born.

Jim's making a plea for us not to vote Labour out as a protest, but to cast a positive vote for change. That's exactly what we're going to do, and that's exactly why we'll be voting to keep Jim's party out of office and to destroy and thoroughly discredit its current leadership and its entire modus operandi. We're doing it out of hope, the scales have fallen from our eyes and we can see the monster Labour has become, dressed in the tattered rags of a party that once stood for the poor, the marginalised, the dispossessed. Modern Labour serves for nothing except itself and a discredited cosy wee establishment that's had it all its own way for far too long. Labour's jockocracy and Uncle Tammery is dead, and in this election Scotland is going to finish it off for good.

Jim bewails the apathy and disengagement he sees in the most politically involved nation in Europe. But it's not that we're not disengaged from politics, we're disengaged from Jim and his politics of passivity, the politics of the little people sitting back quietly and consuming what the likes of Jim tell us the agenda has to be. Fuck that Jim. The political life of a nation is not something we will sit back and lap up while it's dished out to us by the fast food toxicity of the Labour party in Scotland. We'll be telling you what the menu is Jim, we'll set the agenda and you will jump and you will deliver. Or you can put on your jogging pants and jog off. But you jogged off into the twilight a long time ago, it's only now you've just realised that no one has followed you into your dead end.

In Jim Murphy's mental universe the electorate of Scotland is apathetic. That view only serves to show just how hopelessly out of touch the Labour leadership is, trapped in its hall of mirrors, admiring its own reflection and thinking it's being perceptive.

During the independence referendum there was an explosion of political activity from all sorts of people who had never been politically involved in their lives. The referendum taught us that politics is not a spectator sport, it's fun for all the family. To politic is an active verb, a transitive but we are not its objects. We are the agents of change, the medium and the message. The membership figures of the SNP, the Greens and the Scottish Socialists have gone through the roof while Labour withers and dies, the Tories collect their pensions and the Lib Dems go extinct. Non-party organisations flourish, the Common Weal, the National Collective, and a self-made media gives space to voices that were silenced before by the suffocating conformity of a complacent mainstream media. This is Jim's apathy.

The people of Scotland are active agents on their own political stage. We are not Jim's passive consumers, we are not the respectful audience at the play we're not allowed to write. We're the actors, and we're the stars. We're upstaging you Jim. And we will not be getting back into our seats any time soon. Get used to it. We are the future and we're here now.

Vote False Moustache Guy!

7 April 2015

R
ight, here we go the Scottish leaders' debate, or more precisely the five faces of the main parties. That's one each for the Most Dangerous Wummin in Britain, Wee Wullie Rennie and the Action Krankie, and two for Jim Murphy BA Politics (failed). I'm hoping Jim makes an utter tit out of himself, so if you're looking for balanced coverage, go elsewhere. And at this juncture I'd also like to add that it's pure vegetarian mince that Patrick Harvie wasn't invited.

We're getting contributions from the audience, so far we've had one each from supporters of each of the parties. Even the Lib Dems, no really. STV searched far and wide and actually managed to find one who wasn't too embarrassed to appear in public.

Jim is getting asked about why it is that Labour is pure rubbish. How come no one wants to vote for the party any more. Jim's doing that quiet voice thing again. And already I want to throw something at the telly screen. He was upset because a constituent came to him and even though she's got two jobs she still can't afford new shoes for her daughters. According to Jim this is all the fault of the Tories. Jim's got two jobs too. He can afford all sorts of things. His answer to the crying woman is that Labour is going to raise the minimum wage to £8 per hour by 2020. Whoop de doo.

Nicola's turn, and she's laying into both the Tories and Labour. What's the point of a Labour government if all it does is to implement Tory policies? Jim's looking shifty. The camera cuts to a man in the audience picking his nose.

Ruth and Wullie waffled a bit. I couldn't be bothered taking notes. I mean really, what's the point? Sometimes your mind wanders and you find yourself thinking about more productive and useful things, like when did I last defrost the freezer? There's probably a Lib Dem past its sell by date in there somewhere.

Why does Jim Murphy look like a turtle? Oooh he mentioned 1924 as the last time the government was formed by a party that wasn't the largest. Get that biggest party lie in early Jim! Nicola tells him that he needs her help to get Ed Miliband into number 10. I'm still hoping that Jim's going to tell us about someone he met on a train, I like hearing about his fantasy life.

Wullie's getting awfie flustered. He thinks it's wrong that a party that wants to break up Britain should have any say over the UK government. He's not entirely clear why they shouldn't. It's just wrong. He's looking really worried, like he's wondering what time the last bus to Fife is.

Jim mentions football! Yeah! My Jim Murphy bingo scorecard is rapidly filling up. He's still banging on with his biggest party lie, and he mentions 1924 again. It doesn't seem to occur to Jim that he's actually undermining his own point every time he says 1924. The British constitution hasn't changed since 1924.

Thank god, an advert break. So far this debate is really boring. They come back and it's Ruthie taking questions from the audience. I've lost the will to live already. Dear god this audience is dull. Where did STV find these people? We need a heckler in an afghan coat to liven things up. But wait! The cameras cut to a guy with a hat and an obviously fake moustache. Who is fake moustache man? It's the most interesting question of the debate so far. Actually no, it's the only interesting question of the debate so far. He's probably phoned in sick and should be at his work.

Here comes creepy Jim now. Can you tell I'm biased? Good. I wouldn't want anyone to be labouring under any false impressions, unlike Jim. He's staring at the camera like a demented turtle and promising to increase the minimum wage to £8.50 per hour. Oh it's £8.50 an hour that the minimum wage is going to be increased to? When did that happen Jim? You can never be sure with Jim, he just makes up policies as he goes along. Jim is now telling us the polls are "tight". This is a novel interpretation of "the polls say Labour is going to be crushed into dust." Jim gets asked why a small country needs to have nuclear weapons. Jim gives his usual multilateral dodging and doesn't mention the Henry Jackson Society even once.

I still demand to know the identity of fake moustache man. It's far more interesting than anything Jim has to say. The dog has started to bark at the telly. Must be Jim's dog whistles. God this is dull. I think I'll grow a moustache. Do we have to hear from Nicola and Wee Wullie?

Right, Nicola is telling us that the SNP will stand up for Scotland's interests and deliver progressive change, an end to austerity and the bedroom tax, protecting public services. All very good and worthy stuff, but all I can think about is Fake Moustache Guy.

A very dull question from a very dull audience member who is clearly a Tory. He thinks it's insane not to reduce the national debt and wants to know why Nicola isn't in favour of cutting all public spending and imposing a tax on false moustaches. Except of course when the false moustache is worn by a high earner, because they're wealth creators and oh god I want to die now. This guy sounds like the sort of person you get stuck beside on the train and he insists on telling you all about adventures in accountancy for six bloody hours. He needs a false moustache to give him an air of mystery.

She gets asked by a thin lipped guy who really needs a moustache about a second referendum. There's an oooooooh from the "hand-picked by STV" audience as she says that there may, or may not, be a commitment to another referendum in 2016. Nicola retorts that the point is that it's up to the people of Scotland to decide, not politicians. Independence supporting politician supports independence shocker.

Another question about Trident. Nicola says that very few countries have nuclear weapons and they're weapons that can never be used because of the devastation they would cause. She points out that renewing Trident is incompatible with a commitment to multilateral disarmament.

Wee Wullie Rennie is up now. I think it's time to go and make tea, and possibly bake scones and grow a moustache. Seriously, who gives a toss what Wullie has to say? Is there anyone left in the entire country who's going to vote Lib Dem?

Asked why MPs are useless overpaid gits, Wullie says that in four years as an MP he helped 10,000 people with problems. Did he ever attend Parliament? Or was he spending all his days "helping people with problems"? Did any of those problems involve false moustaches? Enquiring minds want to know. False Moustache Guy is polling higher than the Lib Dems.

Where is False Moustache Guy? The cameras must be avoiding him. I miss him. He's the most entertaining thing about this debate so far. He's the only entertaining thing about this debate. If Jim Murphy thought that his performance on this programme was going to turn buoy up the sinking fortunes of the Labour party he's sadly mistaken. He should have worn a false moustache, although admittedly his eyebrows have taken on a life of their own.

That's it. I can't take any more. I've lost the will to live.

Right, we're on the final section now. Thank god it's almost over. This format is dire. It's more dull questions from the dull audience. Sorry audience, but we expect more entertainment from you. More false moustaches and afghan coated heckling please. Jim Murphy seems to contradict what Ed Miliband said last week in his debate, when Ed said that Labour would have to make cuts. Jim says no. Oh god who to believe? Staring eyed Ed or the mad eyebrows of Jim? Nicola nailed him on that point, but trying nail Jim on anything is like trying to stick a blancmange to the wall with a six inch nail.

Jim's promising lots of free things. All sort of free things that he was opposed to just a few short weeks ago. He's promised everything will be free except for false moustaches. He tells a barefaced lie about Labour abolishing tuition fees. Oh Wullie Rennie is still there too. Who realised? Who cares? Jim's conflating devolved and reserved issues again.

This is rubbish STV. Epic fail. I very much doubt whether anyone will have had their mind changed by this debate, or whether anyone will have learned anything that they didn't know already. Those of us who went into the debate thinking Jim was a duplicitous creepy liar will still think he's a duplicitous creepy liar, and those of us who thought that the three Unionist parties would gang up against Nicola Sturgeon were confirmed in our belief.

Jim won't answer Nicola's question - will he vote with the SNP to vote down a Tory Queens Speech if Labour and the SNP combined have more seats than the Tories. Jim refuses to answer, his eyebrows are in overdrive.

Wullie Rennie says, "These are immature games." And on that note, when Wullie Rennie becomes the voice of reason, I'm giving up.